The Shape of the Theological Task

The Shape of the

Theological Task

by

Robert T. Voelkel

The Westminster Press
Philadelphia

Published by The Westminster Press ®
Philadelphia, Pennsylvania

Printed in the United States of America

To Mab
for pins and love

Contents

Preface   9

Introduction   11

Chapter One — Wilhelm Herrmann: German Liberal   17

Herrmann's Use of the Critical Philosophy   19
Religion and the Historical   22
The Communion of the Christian with God   26
Religion and Moral Action   32
Theology Shaped by Faith   38

Chapter Two — The Descendants of Herrmann   44

Theology and the Word of God   45
Word and Faith   53
Jesus and Revelation   59
When to Speak Theologically?   66

Chapter Three — The Shape of Orthodoxy   68

Faith as Life in the New Age and the Johannine
   Provenance   70
The Religious and Intellectual Notions of Illumina-
   tion   77
Creedalism and Political Establishment   82
Theology as Legal Exegesis   87

Chapter Four — Luther and Reformation in Theology   92

    Learning and Human Self-awareness   95
    The Path to Rigid Orthodoxy   100
    Humanism and Religion   106
    Theology Between Rhetoric and Science   112

Chapter Five — Schleiermacher and a New Reformation in Theology   116

    The Essence of Religion and the Theological Task   119
    Tradition and Criticism   126
    The Dilemma of the Theological Professor   131
    Academic Theology in America   137

Chapter Six — The New Shape of the Theological Task   141

    How to Deal with Tradition Untraditionally   145
    The Moral Use of Theological Language   152
    Prognosis   158

    Notes   165

Preface

ONE ENTERS INTO theological discussion in the way he can
and from where he is. The reader of this book will find this not
only evident but in some measure justified. Obviously, I hope
that my utterances are relevant to what other men who do theology find of concern. At the same time I hope that anyone
who is conversant with theological literature will find them helpful. Perhaps it is a vain hope, but still I have it, that literate
men in general will find this work, in spite of its somewhat al-
lusive character, an aid in putting theological work in perspective.

Like every other author, I am in deep debt to those who have
encouraged me and listened patiently to my explorations. This
certainly includes my students who have on more than one occasion glanced through the fog between us and registered recognition. To Robert L. Ferm, J. William Whedbee, and Jack C.
Verheyden, friends and colleagues, I wish to express my deep
gratitude for their careful reading of the manuscript and extremely helpful comments. Where I have been able to make
use of their advice, this book has surely shown improvement.
Where I have not, it probably could be better. To Pomona College and its trustee, Morris B. Pendelton, I wish to express
thanks for funds used for secretarial help. To the Claremont
Graduate School I am indebted for a grant of funds that supported some of the research on Herrmann. To my wife the book
stands in dedication.

R. T. V.

Claremont, California

Introduction

THE CURRENT THEOLOGICAL picture is in need of nothing so much as perspective. Amid the whir of activity in the theological seminaries, amid the flood of publications now made available to more people by the paperback revolution, amid the flourishing of ecclesiastical dialogue and the growing specialization and expertise in scholarship concerning theological matters, and amid the clamor for new ways of saying time-honored things and performing time-honored acts, there is a striking deficiency of those who see the current scene in perspective. For this reason, one who stands somewhat to the edge of institutionalized theology gets the uneasy feeling that much energy is being expended over problems that are neither clearly seen nor worthy of examination. He feels that polemics are misplaced, that arguments are sterile, and that despite its herculean attempt to be relevant, the theological community is becoming increasingly isolated.

Perspective, I would hope, can aid in disengaging one from the particularities of school disputes and by its peculiar view of the relation of things enable him to ask about the real nature of the theological enterprise in order to assess its shape and outline its task. However, to achieve perspective one must rule out from the beginning easy use of the term " theology." For in no area is there greater confusion than in defining what indeed the enterprise is. Thus I shall refrain from arguing immediately about definitions and qualifications and seek, rather, some point of departure that is more specific and less likely to draw us into the beckoning labyrinths.

To find this point of departure is perhaps to find a master key. Nevertheless, it seems rather obvious that we begin with ourselves and work out. What are we as we do theology and how did we get to be as we are? To answer this question we are blessed neither with the possibility of leaping out of our own skins nor with the ability to transcend our own situation. We bump up immediately against the fact that we have been taught to ask questions in specific ways and to select problems for our scrutiny from a common store. We stand on the shoulders of our mentors and naturally face in the direction they have faced, turning this way or that only as a conscious deviation. Thus we must carefully proceed lest we be either too obedient or too rebellious.

At this point we encounter the first difficult hurdle in the quest for perspective. For we live, I would contend, at the end of an age that found its theology shaped by dramatic events and powerful characters. These events were so intense and involved such a commitment of human energy that they gave rise to stylized ways of doing business no longer adequate to our setting. There are strong hints that this age is ending. Bishop Robinson's honesty is one; William Hamilton's waiting for the void to fill up is another; Thomas Altizer's proclamation of the death of God is another; and Harvey Cox's plea for secularity is still another. Beyond them is the growing realization in many quarters that reinterpretation of recent church history and theology may be necessary before clarity is established. However, the power of the giants of the last generation is remarkable. Karl Barth and Rudolf Bultmann still cast long shadows over the current debates in German theology.[1] Paul Tillich remains a towering figure in the world of systematic theology, and his solutions to the age-old problems still commend themselves — even to a dissident like Robinson. In fact, it almost seems as if the giants could well become titans and keep us from seeing them as men who were also shaped by their tutors and who assessed the enterprise in which they were engaged from inside their own skins.

In like manner the events of this century, with its wars, social revolution, and rapid change in international order, may endanger our perspective by looming too large. Do those of us who are involved in doing the business of theology see too closely the coming of wars and depressions and the horrors of a state gone mad, and tend therefore to generalize upon intellectual and theological history too simply? A case in point has to do with theological liberalism, which is identified with political liberalism in the classical sense and with a national and militaristic outlook severely judged by recent European history. The only trouble is that all the connections are tenuous and in certain cases accidental, involving great men in shameful legacies.

All of this brings me to my point of departure. For it is possible, I think, to look at ourselves rather nicely by looking at our teachers through the eyes of their teachers. For me this means going back one generation in German theology to Wilhelm Herrmann, beloved professor of both Barth and Bultmann and one whose work is evidenced not only in their thought but in the shape of contemporary problems. Herrmann is a happy figure to find in our recent past, since he was an extremely gifted theologian, with a type of thought similar to that of his pupils, yet quite different as well. He also demonstrates under scrutiny a remarkable sensitivity to the very problem of perspective that I have posed and will provide, I hope to show, some helpful guidelines in our assessment of the shape of the theological task.

Wilhelm Herrmann lived from 1846 to 1922. His academic career was distinguished by his great success as a teacher. To his classrooms came those who would later establish themselves as greats — the likes of Karl Barth, Rudolf Bultmann, and John Baillie. His writings, though brief, have a lucid style and a simple subtlety of idea. Spending the major part of his career in the university center of Marburg, Herrmann was apprised of the Neo-Kantian revival in philosophy, the new winds of New Testament criticism, and the journalistic leadership in theology of Martin Rade. In conjunction with Rade he edited the famous journal *Zeitschrift für Theologie und Kirche* from 1907 to 1917,[2] and he contributed frequently to *Die christliche Welt* — Rade's attempt to nourish the reading interests of those in the church who wished to transcend simple confessionalism and look at the broader problems of church and culture.

Herrmann's work was known beyond Germany, and he traveled in 1904 to the United States, where he lectured at the University of Chicago.[3] The faculty there saw him as a representative of new and progressive trends. What is so remarkable is that a man of such influence could have been so eclipsed. For there is little evidence that his books were even looked at by the generation of theologians who learned from Barth and his pupils or that Hermann's great fame in any way lasted. Recently his writings have been unearthed and read with interest by a few. Moreover, the *Zeitschrift für Theologie und Kirche* after a lapse of several years was revived in 1950 by Gerhard Ebeling with the specific design of attaching it once again to the best in pre-World War I thought. Herrmann obviously was included in this design. None of this, however, has produced a meaningful Herrmann revival in the theological world at large.[4]

My interest in Herrmann is not merely to do him honor or because I find in his work traces of problems since debated at length. Nor do I wish merely to point out that the lines of continuity between nineteenth- and twentieth-century thought are stronger than those have indicated who rebelled so against the nineteenth century. Rather is it to Herrmann the theologian that I want to direct attention. He was always conscious of exactly the problem that strikes me as neglected today: how the theological task is shaped. He had remarkable perspective on this task, and all his writings are informed by care taken to relate method and content in the theological enterprise.

Of prime importance for this insight which Herrmann had was his knowledge of the ground rules of intellectual life laid down by his own situation in history. He understood that what he was saying was intimately tied up with the way he was saying it and the time and place in which it was said. His reflections on the tradition given to him were always carefully couched to show how he was receiving and molding it. Thus one gets the feeling in reading him that the conclusions to his works are merely temporary pauses in an endeavor that will soon be taken up again in a rather new way. My contention is that such a stance — so rare among theologians — when taken by one so strategically located for those of us who wish to get perspective on our own times must be examined rather carefully as potential help in steadying our ship.

Thus to look at Herrmann, who not only is a teacher as close to our own work as our grandfathers but also an interesting theologian, seems to me to provide the first step in a quest for perspective that will last longer than this short work. In the context of Herrmann's thought we shall ask what theology is to him and gain insight perhaps for what it should be for us.

This essay, therefore, is intended neither as a detailed analysis of Herrmann's thought nor as a study in the recent history of theology. It is, rather, an excursus on Herrmann's thought with interest in furthering our own. As will become apparent, I hope, this is a natural exercise and very beneficial. For, if we allow our thought to move as Herrmann's did, analysis and prescription are one. Moreover, Herrmann understood this unity to come not from thought itself but from the subject matter that the theologian had at hand — the Christian gospel. If this essay succeeds, then, it will be an illustration of its own thesis. For what I wish to argue is that the impulse to theology is a peculiar aspect of the religious tradition deriving from Jesus and his Jewish background. Its crises are at base religious crises and its best moments are moments of religious power. If clarity comes in this small attempt, it reflects custodianship of a rich tradition adequately performed. And if this essay makes its point, the shape of the theological task by being outlined will be reshaped and faith will find a somewhat clearer voice.

CHAPTER ONE

Wilhelm Herrmann: German Liberal

ONE CANNOT READ HERRMANN for very long without being conscious that he wrote his theology as a tract for the times. Living in Germany following unification and reaching the height of his professional career just prior to World War I, Herrmann saw active the forces that in spite of the intervening years of catastrophe continue to shape our culture. Growing prosperity and materialism were all about him. The creeds of nationalism echoed in his ears as the concert of nations gave way to the capricious pursuit of self-interest. A church of some material abundance flourished in a society that looked less and less to it for guidance. And men were drawn closer and closer together by economic and cultural interdependence while being driven farther and farther apart by the happenstance of out-dated political forms.

In the realm of theology Herrmann lived at the close of a century so brilliantly opened by Schleiermacher and Hegel and yet fractured by controversy over establishment in the churches and subscription to orthodox creedal expressions. On the one hand, an intellectual life flowered as the seeds of German Idealism grew. On the other hand, men continued to ask about the validity of time-honored assertions and to look with disfavor upon those who for the good of the society would not submerge their personal difficulties. In Marburg a vigorous school of Neo-Kantians made current a style of thought that although sympathetic to the spiritual grandeur of human life was highly suspicious of the church as custodian of it.

In this context Herrmann addressed himself directly to the problem of faith. If other men were troubled by faith, Herrmann found it the key to the Christian religion and to Christian theology, for in examining faith, Herrmann came to see that it means much more and much different things than its common use would indicate. In fact, it is used carelessly even by those who should know better, as Herrmann so clearly discovered. For when its proper meaning is protected by proper use, the conception of faith becomes the thin red line that runs through Christianity denoting its essence. Faith extends from Jesus, through Paul and the New Testament, to Christian piety everywhere. Luther knew this as almost no other did, thought Herrmann, and in this way he sought always to identify with the great Reformer.

In this fashion the apologetic and constructive tasks became the same for Herrmann. His tracts for the times could be full-blown theological works as well. Part of his genius is that amid the conciseness and simplicity of his style one finds these two never separated. His writings show the hand of the craftsman, but they also show that he had discovered in examining faith that to be an apologist need not put one on the defensive. Instead, it makes it possible for him to face the burden of modern critical work on the Christian tradition without the fear that this will undermine the foundations of the Christian religion. Rather, he can announce that with these critical labors faith will be free to exercise its power.

This attempt to stand as defender of the faith and modern man brought Herrmann into controversies on the right and on the left. His deftness is seen in his ability to tread the razor's edge, falling to neither side. For he saw in both the demands of the orthodox that he adhere to traditional creedal statements as the object of faith and in the demands of rational theologians of *Religionsphilosophie* that religion be justified in the realm of general science a common misunderstanding of faith. Whether this might come from subsuming it to traditional dogma or encasing it in the bounds of reason alone, its reality would be lost in the process.

Defense, however, always led in Herrmann's case to counter-attack. Thus he consciously sought to bring his loyalty to Luther and the sources of faith in the New Testament into conjunction with a way informed by Kant for arguing his case in the modern world. He had explored Kant to the fullest and wrote easily and clearly in Kantian terms. His deftness is illustrated by the way he called upon Kant for help in demolishing the traditionalists while calling upon Luther to escape Kant.

At all times, however, Herrmann remained consistent in his aim. He was a systematic theologian, and his early and large work, *Religion in Relation to Knowledge of the World and Morality* — which more than any other work of his argued philosophical themes — was subtitled *A Foundation for Systematic Theology*. Faith led to theology, but in that order, and this becomes crucial for an understanding of Herrmann. His intellectual pursuits always flowed from that reality which was essential to the Christian gospel. This in no way compromised his academic stance, but it kept aims and purposes clear. These purposes which he followed assiduously not only shaped his theology but allowed him to shape the theological task.

HERRMANN'S USE OF THE CRITICAL PHILOSOPHY

The writings of the church — which form the bulk of theological discourse — have shared with many other writings an impulse to find in their own expressions that which has universal claim upon men and may be seen as the ultimate clue to the nature of things. This impulse is not lacking in the various attempts from Origen onward to set out a systematic account of the world and man in it which depends for its substance upon the special proclamation of the Christian gospel. It is further to be found in the claims made for Christian dogmatic formulas, especially by those who claim to represent orthodoxy. These latter Herrmann called traditionalists.

The endeavor of a traditionalist is rather like that of every science which strives for universal validity, but its scope really compares most accurately with metaphysics. In both, claims are made about the world, man, and perhaps God, beyond which there is no greater appeal. To both, Kant thought he had delivered the death blow in his critical philosophy, and Herrmann agreed. For Kant saw in these comprehensive claims a misunderstanding of human reasoning which produced them. He sought to show, at least as Herrmann read him, that correcting this misunderstanding necessitated taking into account the concerns of the one who reasons.

What Kant brought correctly to light, Herrmann thought, was that the process of knowledge, proceeding as it does to appropriate the order and lawfulness of reality, finds this order not in the world which it meets but in the presuppositions of the reasoning process itself.[1] Representations that are brought to consciousness in the act of knowledge describe relationships that are found in experience. Pure reason, the inventive and speculative aspect of the mind, traces out the components of these representations and seeks to explore possibilities of combining the parts and whole. In this action of pure reason new representations are born and these proliferate at varying speeds. If pure reason were all there is to reasoning, this proliferation would be unending.

It is the practical concern of the man who reasons which puts a limit to this activity. Thus he counts as significant and uses only those representations which help him come to terms with reality as he meets it in the experiences of his life. The interplay of one's own being and the world in which he lives determine in large measure the life of the mind. The activities of pure reason and the aims and purposes of a specific man are balanced against one another as he goes to meet the demands of the moment. In the process pure reason is chastened.

The implications of this critical study for the propositions of traditional theology are clear and devastating. Not only are the proofs for the existence of God — the so-called necessary truths of reason — rendered ineffective; the content of theological assertions is placed in the no-man's-land of relativity. They become merely representations reflective not of reality in itself but of the orientation of a man to his world. Since Kant, says Herrmann, no one can claim universal validity for the representations of reality that are real to his own experience. To be sure, the problem of universal validity remains. But its solution must lie outside metaphysics and its partner, traditional orthodoxy.

Kant located morality and the search for the moral law whereby the will might be guided as the area where universal validity is a relevant notion. Here one searches for a way of showing that his actions, if they are good, are motivated not merely by whim or by habit but by an initiation that might truly be called free. He seeks to transcend the particular moment of his moral action and place his decisions in the context of the universal. Thus the field that was preempted by metaphysics is claimed for ethics.

In like manner Herrmann claims that the reasoning process because of its being attuned to the demands of one's particular existence connects the drive for universal validity with judgments of value in moral action. By no means does anyone escape the drive for universal validity. However, if he pursues it in the direction of metaphysics in the classical sense, he is caught pursuing the forlorn hopes of pure reason. Even a metaphysics of morals can never escape the dilemma, since the drive to transcend the particular moment of moral decision can never succeed. In this respect, Herrmann can be said to out-Kant Kant.

Where now does one turn in the quest for universal validity if he agrees with Herrmann that metaphysics even in its limited sense cannot succeed? The only alternative open, Herrmann argues, is religion, where the necessity of justifying universal claims in the realm of science is not called for. Rather, the call to moral action with a claim of universality arises from something other than man's reasoning. Is it a mystical awareness? Here Herrmann is most troubled, and it is mysticism, not traditionalism or rationalism, that he finds his most serious contender. He says that it is not a mystical awareness but faith. However, he allows that mysticism is most dangerous because it resembles faith so nearly.

What is faith? Before that question can be answered another tack must be taken in approaching the question of universal validity and historical relativity. In short, we must see how Herrmann takes up Lessing's question.

RELIGION AND THE HISTORICAL

Lessing had wondered how one could say that the accidental truths of history could be a sufficient basis for the necessary truths of reason. Or in our paraphrase: How can that which claims universal validity rest upon the relative occurrence of historical events? For Lessing, the question arose as he sought to find some basis for attaching special importance to the Christian tradition. He has become for this reason the paradigm of the problem faced by any modern Christian theologian.

Herrmann addressed himself to this problem in a lecture delivered in Marburg on March 22, 1884, in honor of the birthday of Kaiser Wilhelm I.[2] It is characteristic of him that such an occasion called for theological analysis, but it is noteworthy that he would see in the figure of the Prussian king become German emperor the problem of historical relativity and universal validity.

In this speech, which is colored by German nationalism, Herrmann argues that the people of Germany owe the Kaiser a debt of gratitude for bringing them together and giving them a destiny as a people. His royal personage now signifies a common dedication of his subjects; through him they have become a *Volk*. However, Germany has had another tradition that must be given its due — the tradition of its universities and its science. And in this tradition the particular destiny of a people is of little consequence. In science, appeal is not to race or background but to truth conceived as the universally valid. How, suggests Herrmann, can the people of Germany be honest to both? They cannot live forever politically divided, hearing from the French that their national role is to be the schoolhouse of nations. They must know the unity and purpose of national identity. Yet they must defend the great tradition of learning, the search for truth apart from its political basis, and the objective detachment of wisdom.

Here Herrmann turns to Lessing's question. What he says can be very illuminating in seeing his way beyond Kant. Lessing, says Herrmann, was experiencing in his own day what the German of the late nineteenth century was in his. As the latter found within himself the drive to national unity at odds with yearning to be one with eternal truth or timeless expressions of beauty, so did Lessing experience a tension between his identification with the Christian tradition and the demands of enlightened men that each particular part of human history justify itself by the canons of science. In the political sphere, argues Herrmann, the dilemma has more urgency, for to abdicate the demands of historical life in a particular community is to find this community relegated by others to a particular style of life.[3] Thus is it indeed for the German who is looked down upon by the French. He finds self-justification and restoration of purpose in the events of 1870 and the leadership of the Kaiser. For Lessing, the dilemma was more subtle but no less real.

Lessing could find no way out of this dilemma, claims Herrmann; it was " the great abyss " which he could not cross. But he at least was troubled by the need to be part of a historical tradition. Kant, on the other hand, refused to see in history a problem. Rather did one strive to get straight the facts only when the truths of history were at stake. It was merely a question of knowledge, and for one who was interested in religion, nothing appropriate was to be found here. To be sure, Kant saw Christianity arising in a particular historical context, but he attached no great significance to this. Instead, he wished to clear the ground for faith by detaching it from the situation in which new discoveries of fact might destroy it.[4]

Herrmann argues that Kant wished to see faith as trust in the moral law. This law has a universal validity which stands prior to the exercise of reason, since it conditions fundamentally the process of valuation that is involved. What is missing is any explanation of why one should trust the moral law. What is the motivation of a human person toward faith? And here, thought Herrmann, Kant was blind to something that Lessing saw clearly. For the historical cast of the Christian religion brings a man a particular demand for faith in the presence of a particular religious community. The question of motivation, therefore, is attached to a very particular case of a man's being motivated. Lessing saw the great importance of this and wished not to leave it quickly behind. At the same time he was sensitive to the demands of reason which bring to any specific case the requirement of universal validity. But he remained stuck here while Kant pressed on to a metaphysic of morals.

Now, one might argue that Kant's explication of the moral law and his inferences drawn from it are in large measure conditioned by his own historical context and are not wholly unrelated to the Christian tradition in which he was raised. Herrmann chose rather to argue that a theoretical mistake had been made when Kant sought to find the locus of consciousness and hence of man's decision-making in examining subjectivity and not personality. Hence, he could make the whole set of problems that revolve around freedom, willing, and the good adjuncts to the problems of epistemology.

By shifting the locus of human origination to personality or personhood (*Persönlichkeit*) Herrmann wished to take more sufficient stock of the fact that a person is the counterpart of a particular set of historical circumstances. He says:

> We call a man a person in so far as he has not only consciousness but directly senses value in an experience and believes himself to possess in his willing the ability to realize

this value. Inseparable from a person is the representation of
a certain movement of the world since without the conviction
of the reality of this world and its course his own existence
with its inalienable claims must appear to him to be senseless.[5]

Person (or self) and world form the poles of decision and
describe the conditions in which reasoning and knowledge take
place. Reality is not the correlative of knowledge as this takes
place in consciousness but of a person as he acts in history.
Or, in more Kantian language: " The thing-in-itself is not the
correlative of the subject which is certain of its existence in
direct awareness." [6]

It is obvious that Herrmann has here learned from Schleiermacher, and this fact of his thought will concern us when the
time comes. However, it must be noted that Herrmann wished
to keep his distance from Schleiermacher as well as from Kant.
For both of them, he thought, finally avoided Lessing's question. Both of them sought the eternal in separation from the
historical; the universal even though connected with the historical transcended it. Whereas Kant turned to a metaphysic
of morals, Schleiermacher came dangerously close to mysticism. And this made him more open to suspicion and more
prone to find the locus of religious life outside the concrete
demands of existence in the historical and hence beyond
personality.

What Herrmann wished to separate carefully were the problems of nature and history. In the former, one is concerned
with relationships that can be depended upon to prevail — with
laws. These need not be part of an all-inclusive unity; in fact,
this aim of traditional metaphysics has been ruled out by critical philosophy. They need only form consistent patterns which
may then be used to solve particular problems. When one is
concerned with history, however, he needs not theoretical unity
but the unity of purpose. He becomes a person as he wills and
acts — in short, as he makes history. In theology, metaphysics
and mysticism are reflective of concentration on nature —
either as science or as art. Both, however, are alien to faith.

For faith as the peculiar and specific essence of the Christian religion not only is tied up with a particular historical tradition, it is also realized only by one whose concern is historical. It is only distorted when spoken about in terms appropriate to nature.

At this point we can wait no longer to explore the meaning of faith as Herrmann sees this arising in the Christian religion and forever defining its true character.

THE COMMUNION OF THE CHRISTIAN WITH GOD

In 1886, Herrmann published *The Communion of the Christian with God* — a book that was to go through seven editions and remains the one most representative of his thought. Characteristically, he moves from a discussion of the ills of doctrinal orthodoxy through a critique of mysticism to an explication of how Christian faith arises and issues forth in moral action.

Faith arises, says Herrmann, not in the acceptance of propositions of doctrine but in encounter with the influence of Jesus as this is present in historical Christianity. This influence is such that one finds himself brought face to face with the living God directly and powerfully. However, an encounter of this nature demands that one be called to a full possession of himself in which he speaks and acts as only he in his particular situation can. If he is to express his faith, it must be for himself and from himself. The result is that anything which is alien to his person is not only irrelevant but detrimental to faith. To think of superimposing statements of doctrine which are without meaning upon a man who is coming to faith is to think of aborting the whole process. The reality of faith and uniformity of doctrine are mutually exclusive. " The true objectivity of Christian knowledge, its truth for believers, must be lost unless it is protected by clear views concerning the life of faith." [7]

Now, to be sure, speaking about the influence of Jesus involves one in the sticky business of indicating just what this influence is, what place the Christian tradition has in it, and how doctrinal orthodoxy may be alien. But it is Herrmann's intention to deal with questions of this nature, for at the heart of his thought stands the figure of Jesus. In fact, he goes on to argue that the key failure of mysticism is its misuse of the Christ as a means to mystic union with the ineffable God. This he claims, is the major flaw in Roman Catholic piety, the correction of which is integral to Protestantism. The mystic, although he may subscribe to the most orthodox of formulas about the Christ and although he may phrase the description of his ascent in highly Christological terms, does in the last analysis seek refuge beyond the historical and specific figure of Jesus in eternal union with Deity itself.

To do so, Herrmann claims, is to throw all of the theological machinery out of balance. No idea of God, no proper understanding of faith, no retention of the essence of Christian experience is possible if the figure Jesus is transcended. But to keep from doing this is extremely difficult, for it is not only in the abstract dogmas of Christology that Jesus is left behind. Use of traditional descriptions of his life as examples for piety or action also abandons the historical character of Jesus and turns him into an archetype. He becomes again a means to another end. Such, however, is not the place Jesus has in the Christian religion.

> The Christian has a positive vision of God in the personal life of Jesus Christ. This vision of God does actually set us free from the world, because it leads us to deny self, and is grasped and realised only in connection with moral impulse. We are guided, however, to this condition neither by the Church's dogmas concerning Christ, nor yet by using Jesus' human life as our example. We cannot enter fully into the same relation to God which Jesus had; that remains his own secret. But we can enter into the relation to God into which the redemption of Christ brings us only if, in our finding of God, we do not lose sight of Jesus. It is just here that both the doctrine of the Church and the use of the life of Jesus as an example prove insufficient. For the man who has nothing more of Christ than these two things must leave Christ all behind when once there awakes in him that genuine religious

impulse which will be satisfied with nothing but God alone. How can he stay with Christ if he looks upon Him as only a condition, a way and means whereby to come to God? He must break through everything (even though it be adorned with the name of God like the Christ of ecclesiastical dogma) which serves only as a means, and is thus utterly different from the God whom we must find in the highest flight that our religious life attains.

Here is the limit beyond which that conception of Christ, which is embodied in the dogma and practice of Roman Catholicism, does not rise; the Christ thus conceived cannot be taken in with the soul into the inmost experiences of the religious life. When this kind of Christianity attains its goal, although it is borne forward by the most genuine religious impulse, it is de-christianized. We must get past the old dogma of the Deity of Christ to a higher conception of Christ, one which does not compel us to leave Him outside when we take religion, that is the communion of the soul with God, in all earnestness and truth.[8]

This higher conception of Christ which does justice to his influence in Christian religious experience and provides for a proper view of communion with God comes when one understands the fully personal character of faith. And despite the attitude we might take toward Herrmann's anti-Roman Catholic polemics, it is certainly true that he correctly understood here the basis of Luther's rebellion.[9] The fact that Luther adhered strictly to the traditional doctrines about Christ need not turn one away from the fact that he found himself captive to Christ in a way which was absolutely crucial to his being and that this brought him into conflict with the authority of the church. His faith and his person were inseparable.

This personal character of faith Herrmann accounts for by speaking of the power exercised upon a man by the inner life of Jesus — a power that is inseparable from his becoming a self. Thus the encounter with Jesus is a historical encounter. That is to say that it takes place in the history of the man of faith and it comes into being in the context of a particular historical community. Jesus as the founder of this community and the source of the religious impulse contained in its tradition remains historical as well. Obviously we are now at a very delicate point in the fabric of Herrmann's thought approaching Lessing's question and also opening that of the historical Jesus. Of the latter, Herrmann was not ignorant, since he became embroiled in debate with Martin Kaehler over this issue and was very conscious of the problems being raised in New Testament studies.

In dealing with the New Testament, one is confronted with the problem of making historical judgments which are of only probable validity and which may be overturned by continuing scholarly labor. This need not, however, cause one to be skeptical about the figure of Jesus to the point where he ceases to exercise religious influence.

> Here Lessing is right. If, notwithstanding all this, the person of Jesus is so certainly a fact to us Christians that we do see in Him the basis of our faith, and the present revelation of God to us, this conviction is not produced by historical judgment. The calmness with which Christendom holds by the historical reality of Jesus has certainly not been won by the forcible suppression of historical doubt. Any such effort would be made contrary to the dictates of conscience, and it could give no man peace. It is something quite different which removed all doubt from the picture of Jesus; if we have that picture at all, we have it as the result, not of our own efforts, but of the power of Jesus Himself.[10]

This something quite different is the true historical (*geschichtlich* rather than *historisch* if one must succumb to current convention) understanding of the power of Christ found where the inner life of Jesus is presently of influence. And this happens in the church as it presently lives. " We need communion with Christians in order that, from the picture of Jesus which His church has preserved, there may shine forth that inner life which is the heart of it. It is only when we see its effects that our eyes are opened to its reality so that we thereby experience the same effect." [11]

In other words, the student of the New Testament makes a

grievous error if he tries to skip from the New Testament to present-day faith without taking stock of the lines of continuity that run through the history of the church and that derive their force from the continuing religious impulse of Jesus. When they do, the technical problems of New Testament research may not be solved but they will be seen as parts of a larger question in the history of religion revolving around the real nature of Christian experience.

To arrive at this point is to examine the figure of Jesus in relationship to redemption, for the power of the inner life of Jesus known in the life of the church draws one out of the mere circumstances of his existence and into personal freedom. This is salvation, and its source in Jesus is the saving fact. No one will understand this, of course, who is not himself aware of salvation, and no amount of arguing questions of historical fact will help.

> The only thing of importance is to elevate above everything else that present experience in which we and others feel that the power of Jesus really exercises an inward compulsion upon us and lifts us out of ourselves. Therefore we abandon the thoughtless habit of simply saying to men that they must see the saving facts in things that they can grasp only as the contents of other people's stories. For only something which inwardly transforms him can constitute a saving fact for a man who wishes to rise out of his spiritual weakness. And this effect can be exercised on a person only by something he has himself experienced, and not by something that is merely told him. Therefore, we call the inner life of Jesus the saving fact.[12]

From this point of view, Herrmann argues, a whole new vista for viewing history is opened up to the man who has experienced salvation. In relationship to Jesus the person of one who takes possession of himself and devotes himself completely to his mission becomes conceivable. Furthermore, one sees Jesus' messianic consciousness — which Herrmann acknowledges — as the direct result of his own understanding that he is to call men to face the imminent coming of God's full sovereignty in the Kingdom.

But this is not the end of the matter. For such an understanding of history takes place only when one knows himself called to a life in his own history which manifests this impulse. In Luther's words he becomes a Christ to his neighbor. The enduring agency of this impulse and the body whose life is only intelligible in the light of it is the church. In the church, to use Melanchthon's words, to know Christ is to know his benefits.

It should now be obvious why Herrmann makes such a concerted attack upon mysticism. For the attempt to transcend the historical leads one to expect that the peculiar nature of his historical experience is not germane to his salvation. Indeed, the opposite is the case. His salvation is a reality only if his personal existence is realized under the impact of religious impulses beginning with Jesus and living on in the church. Jesus as the Christ is never merely a means to union with the Deity. The nature of Deity is known only in the particular existence of the believer.

It also should be obvious at this point why Herrmann so distrusted those who would require subscription to creeds and who saw faith as affirmation of dogmatic propositions. Faith must depend upon the individuality of the one who has it or it is not faith. Trust and confidence in God come only when one is called to personal integrity. Faith indeed is " the deep awareness of God's influence which forces upon us a new way of thinking, feeling, and willing and allows us to see the world in which we live in a new light." [13] What is this other than what Paul would have called " life in the Spirit "?

If to be called to be a self with unity of purpose in history is faith, the consequence of this is finding a certain unity in one's world. This is not a metaphysical unity but a unity whereby one may say, " God has made this world and it is good." In this world he finds himself in a position to make moral judgments and exercise moral discretion. In taking possession of himself (*Selbstbesinnung*) he has a moral disposition (*Gesinnung*) and a conscience.

At this point we must explore more fully the way in which faith issues in moral action. For here Herrmann's deviations from Kant become most meaningful.

RELIGION AND MORAL ACTION

Herrmann's other major work was his *Ethik* — a volume never translated into English. It takes up in a rather different way the themes that occupy the last half of *The Communion of the Christian with God,* and this literary occurrence is interesting evidence of the connection that Herrmann always made between the essence of Christian religious experience in faith and in moral action. Once again in Pauline terms: faith for Herrmann was always faith active in love.

In taking up the question of ethics, Herrmann indicates that it is a question characteristic of human life and a clue to life's fundamental nature. For what makes a man a man is a process whereby he sees his actions not solely as the product of his surroundings and in which he seeks to root these actions in something that is universally binding for all men. On the one hand, then, ethics involves the question of one's individual selfhood, and on the other, it requires the universally valid.

In terms that echo Kant he goes on to argue that the question of ethics itself is part of this process in which one becomes conscious of his own existence as a living being over and above and yet including the material stuff involved. In fact, the question of ethics is really the most radical question that occurs to a man, for it refuses to be reduced to some other question. It demands that the individuality of man and his self-consciousness not be accounted for in any other terms than free decision and responsible action. Hence, ethics in its proper sense is not the study of history or of human culture. It is an analysis of the way one commands himself and wills. The presupposition here involved is that one's willing is irreducible, and this separates ethics from its cleverest and most serious rival — psychology. For it denies that even an analysis of the peculiar character of human responsiveness is sufficient to deal with selfhood as this is concretely realized.

Herrmann supports his views on the nature of ethics by showing that the study of ethics arose in the Western intellectual tradition with the attempt to distinguish human motivation from a mere response to custom and has progressed to the point where one asks about the disposition of a man with a good will. The Sophists were the first to insist that one should act not merely according to custom but in accord with his nature. Although this did not sufficiently clarify the ethical question, since it left the distinction between custom and nature unclear, it was a necessary prelude to Plato, who for the first time asked about the principles in connection with which one distinguishes that which is truly his nature from appearance.

No one until Kant really appreciated the profundity of Plato's question, Herrmann says, for from Aristotle onward a notion of the relationship between human self-realization and nature prevailed which threatened to make man as much a slave to nature and fate as he had been to custom. Even Aristotle, however, contributed an important dimension to the question of ethics by indicating that it is essentially a question of man's *eudaimonia*. When one considers his happiness or well-being, it cannot be without reference to his individual being. Nevertheless, Aristotle because he saw one's well-being so closely connected with his fate provided an ethics that was really " an exposition of the prudent life lived by a finely cultured and well situated man." [14]

What Herrmann wished to do in his *Ethik* was to return to Plato's question of how the good and the true are connected. This can be done, however, only if one realizes that Plato did not formulate this question quite right. One should ask not for the nature of the good but for what is fundamental in a good will. Then one does justice to the concern with *eudaimonia*. For well-being, if it be that of a person who has integrity and continuity through time, is more than just reaction to momentary pleasure and pain. It relates rather to a complex set of calculations and decisions defined by this person's end purposes. Happiness comes only to one who by his good will is true to himself.

The question of a good will brings us back once more to the distinction between nature and history, for in the latter, individuality and uniqueness of purpose are of importance while in the former, patterns and correspondences are. And it is here that Herrmann explores again what is involved in man's historical life.

Life in history involves a man in human community and brings about an expression of human life dependent upon personal interchange. In the context of his fellows one experiences trust in connection with which others become not just the furniture of his world but independent beings who have value by virtue of their particular ways of shaping and molding the things around them. Furthermore, they bring out in other individuals similar skills. This experience is basically trust, since it eludes any certainty which we might call proof. Another's individuality may not be reliable, but personal interchange requires that we take it to be — at least in some measure. In fact, violations of trust are dependent upon our expectations that the other will not violate trust and therefore evidence of trust's precedence. And the relative freedom from circumstances that is so characteristic of personal life is born of trust even in — indeed almost by virtue of — its violation. Finally, it is in trust that one feels within himself an " ought " whereby he responds not of necessity but from a sense of responsibility.

Thus it is in human community and in the experience of trust which is so basic to it that one finds himself raised above the mere animal in himself, made aware of history, and faced with the ethical question. " We can only understand moral thoughts if we have experienced for ourselves the event which becomes possible through them alone. In this event of trust begins always anew truly human life distinguishing itself from nature — or, history. These thoughts, in their power to shape the human, form the sole object of ethics." [15]

Here Herrmann acknowledges that it was Kant more than any other who understood the ethical question. For Kant saw that the moral law cannot be found unless one takes full stock of the dimensions of personal freedom. The moral law is properly not a prescription for judgments but a prescription for the process of making judgments. Kant's categorical imperative was just this. Herrmann goes on to claim that the real intent behind this particular formulation was to take account of the historical existence of particular men who face particular decisions and to allow them exactly the freedom which is necessary for a historical being. It would be in accord, then, with Kant's intent if we rendered his formulation of the moral law insufficient and pressed on to one which more adequately than his comes to terms with the nature of historical existence.

Since Herrmann sees human community as the prerequisite and setting for human self-realization, he reformulates the moral law thus: " We should in each moment make this the norm of our behavior: You should base your entire existence on reaching the deepest and farthest reaching community with other men; and add immediately: You should be innerly independent and thereby truly living." [16]

The universal validity or truth of the moral law is found exactly in its demand that one be not the product of his circumstances but that he exercise lordship over them. It extends beyond the concerns of the present moment, even though one can know it in his own experience only in intimate relationship with the particular aspects of his own existence.

History is the only place where the moral law can be understood, for it is in the moral demand that one becomes clearly conscious of past, present, and future. One is called out of the past into free expression now in order to help shape the novelty of the future. To exist as the product of one's past is to become subject to fate or be reduced to a being controlled by nature. To know the unique possibilities of human life in the future is to share in their actualization. This contributes to the richness of human community and actually expands the possibilities of others. Moreover, moral life is preserved in this way, since it remains constantly the demand of the present moment and at no time becomes the moral achievements of the past. Growth and development are concepts that are necessary to deal adequately with moral experience, but the most important concept is personality.

It is in personality that Herrmann's various avenues of thought intersect. For to experience the moral demand is to be a person who has a history and knows himself called to be independent of the natural conditions in which he is placed. But it is also to know that the secret of one's own existence is unveiled only when one feels the demand to be a responsible human being. Death, for example, as the final and unavoidable claim of natural life upon us looms large only when we realize the burden of freedom. But then in obedience to the moral law death is swallowed up by the abundant source of life itself. The future, which is opened up in moral life with all its novelty and uncertainty, provides a vista beyond the burdens of finitude.

It is in exploring the makeup of personality and its connection with moral experience that Herrmann departs from Kant. But he has followed Kant very far. He has agreed with the critical philosophy that one must clearly delineate the spheres in which certain conceptions have functional value. And by this means he has discussed good and evil not in connection with nature or metaphysics but in connection with history and human willing. However, like Kant he is aware that nature and fate are not easily discarded. Insistence upon the dignity of man in the freedom of moral action does not push aside the fact that men often are not free and often suffer bondage to fate. In other words, like Kant, Herrmann faces the problem of radical evil. However, it is here that he departs from Kant most markedly and where he brings morality and religion together so differently.

Herrmann acknowledges that one does not automatically have the future opened to him by the demands of the moral law. He does not automatically come to experience history in

human community. Trust by its very character does not come naturally. Something comes to one from outside, drawing him into trust and opening for him the possibilities of the future. And here trust is related to faith. For in fact the experience of faith is exactly one of being drawn into trust — a personal experience which is accompanied by a sense of deliverance or forgiveness. Almost as a reflex action but certainly as part of the experience is a sense of guilt as one in coming to responsibility is aware of the burden of the past. He knows how fate and nature can hold him captive. Hence, radical evil is known only by the one who has come to know the moral demand.

Faith comes to be as the influence of Jesus is felt in the Christian community where trust is fostered and where the inner life of Jesus is kept alive. Here concretely and specifically moral life lives also as the impulses to have a good will are passed on. Salvation as this comes from the Redeemer awakens one to the possibilities of his own history and his responsibility in effecting them. And in this context the awareness of how radical evil is can be articulated in the consciousness of sin and guilt.

Anyone whose ear is attuned to the themes of Luther surely hears them here. The helpless sinner is justified by grace in faith alone and is thereby empowered to become a Christ to his neighbor. As the radical nature of sin and the complete ineffectiveness of good works go hand in hand with an overwhelming sense of the goodness of God's grace, so also are religion and moral action united.

Moreover, whereas Kant had brought religion into the bounds of reason alone and been stumped by radical evil, Herrmann finds moral action inexplicable apart from religious impulse in a particular religious tradition. Here he pays tribute to Lessing's labors and hopes to have answered Lessing's question. Universal validity comes not in a transcendental exercise of reason but in the posture of trust whereby one looks outside himself to the community of men as the assemblage of moral persons.

THEOLOGY SHAPED BY FAITH

Our purposes in surveying Herrmann's thought will be fulfilled only if we see how it affected his work as a systematic
theologian. Happily, he followed through the implications of his
treatment of faith consistently. In the process, theology became
something quite distinctive.

First of all, Herrmann wanted to take stock of the relationship between the verbal and intellectual formulations arising in
the Christian tradition and faith, which is the Christian religion's essence. This is not an easy exercise, since faith taking
place in the encounter between human beings involves speech
and thought. One must begin by looking through the eyes of
the historical critic at the development of the Christian religion and its dogma. And for this reason, dogma forms the object not of systematic theology but of its historical partner.
" For with us there cannot be a systematic but only a historical
science of dogma, since Evangelical Christianity cannot have
any dogmas in the old sense of the term." [17] But if one brings
into play the whole notion of history which Herrmann has so
carefully developed, then he knows that study of the life of the
Christian community to be accurate must involve one in the
power of faith. Thus to articulate correctly past verbal and intellectual expressions of faith is to make them intelligible and
moving today. Nothing less than this is either historically or
theologically adequate.

Now, it is true that this point of view is closely related to
Herrmann's ideas about the essence of the Christian religion
and the place of Jesus in it. But he is quite prepared to argue
the case in these terms and see where it leads. In other words,
he is willing quite easily to leave methodological questions and
turn to questions of substance. And this is especially the case
if the questions of substance involve the figure of Jesus. For
one must remember that it is precisely in connection with the
figure of Jesus that he mounts his attack upon both mysticism
and traditional doctrinal orthodoxy.

In these attacks Herrmann had made clear that he saw traditional orthodoxy and mysticism using the figure of Jesus as a means to an end. In the former case this involved the transmutation of faith into assent to doctrinal propositions; in the latter, it necessitated leaving Jesus behind for a union with God himself. In neither case did the peculiar influence of Jesus as the founder of the Christian religion and its sustainer get proper treatment. And the result was the production of a Jesus who was not historical either in his own day or in ours. He became the subject of intellectualized religion fixed to a particular period in church history or an archetype available for *imitatio.*

This same sort of misreading of the figure of Jesus is to be found in connection with moral action. The words of Jesus are lifted out of their historical context and made into codes or principles that must be adhered to by the Christian. The so-called " counsels of perfection " which stand so closely to the bases of monasticism are really Jesus' words misread. Luther's great insight in abandoning monasticism and directing his polemic against it was founded upon his realization that Jesus' real demand for obedience was not so honored. It was instead a demand addressed to every man who met him and had to be understood in terms of this encounter. Thus Luther unfolded his whole doctrine of vocation — a man is called in the place in creation where God has stationed him. Luther did not, however, have the tools for adequately interpreting Jesus' demand for obedience, and Protestantism merely followed the Roman Catholic pattern in its Biblicism.

Herrmann goes on in this argument to conclude that the division between clergy and laity in both communions flows directly from this error in interpreting Jesus and leads to the institutional aberrations which involve conflict between the secular and sacred orders — including those between church and state.[18] However, to pursue this facet of the argument would involve us in a staggering job of church history.

Focusing upon the nature of Jesus' demand for obedience leads us right back to faith. It forces us to ask ourselves what gave his demand for obedience the power that men experienced in their lives and have communicated to other men from that day on. In other words, the repetition of Jesus' address to the men of his day is not sufficient to produce the obedience he was asking. Rather, one must find the source of Jesus' authority in the inner life which was his alone to have but which drew others to a personal freedom individual to them, and through them and their successors continues to awaken faith.

Here Herrmann has occasion to consider the work of Johannes Weiss which appeared so threatening. Does Weiss's demonstration that Jesus' preaching of the Kingdom of God was eschatologically conditioned, and really had nothing to do with an earthly kingdom to be realized by the work of Christians, actually weaken the moral demand found in this preaching? No, argues Herrmann, for now one can see more clearly than ever that his moral demand is dependent upon the moral power of his personality and obedience is a personal response of the man of faith.

Although it seems that Herrmann did not consider some of the further implications of Weiss's work which are now commonplace to the student of New Testament criticism, and although he seemed to find available in the Gospels a literary presentation of Jesus' personality which was commanding, the substance of his argument may be retained. Regardless of how far removed the Synoptic presentation of Jesus may be from his own personal influence, one must account for the power of faith that derives from Jesus. His personal secret may be an even greater secret than Herrmann imagined. But its unveiling still comes only to each one who finds in the living faith of the Christian religion his own personal secret.

In his lectures on systematic theology Herrmann tried to explicate in order three moments in the verbal expression of faith. The order is of great importance, for this is not just a descriptive exercise. Personal life is so bound up with verbal expression that faith will be violated if the sequence of statements is misconstrued. First of all, he shows how " we overcome the world in the consciousness of God's working through Christ." Secondly, he deals with sin and God's gracious gift which overcomes it. And then finally he shows " how in consequence we conceive of the historical facts by which we are thus transformed: (1) the Person of Jesus; (2) the Spirit working in the community. At the end of the course the knowledge of the Nature of God which is implied in this divine activity will be summed up in the Christian doctrine of the Trinity." [19] In all of this the experience of faith is brought to as actual an expression as possible.

Under these three headings Herrmann takes up many of the classical theological issues, but his discussion brings them subject to the essential religious experience of faith. He is by no means obligated to discuss all the classical problems, for some of them seem to him really irrelevant or useless. Furthermore, he is willing to be critical if he must of time-honored and canonically authoritative formulas. As example, since it is pertinent to his Christocentric orientation, we may select his treatment of two-nature Christology. It comes in that section of the lectures in which Herrmann traces out what can be said about the nature of God implied in the divine activity of grace.

God, he says, is known as Father in Biblical language, for we experience in faith as this comes from Jesus " the basis of our confidence and moral end. God is, then, the Creator of our inner life or of our real self. That is what Jesus meant when he called God our Father." [20] There is no more adequate language for describing the place of Jesus in this experience than calling him " Son of God " — regardless of problems involved in this terminology. It is further correct to assert as was done at Nicaea that Jesus is *homoousios* with the Father, since this protects the fundamental character of faith. There is no sort of demigod involved in the act of salvation, but that which is basic to our existence. Furthermore, the place of Jesus in the experience of faith is not something accidental to what ultimately defines our purposes; without Jesus there is no Christian religion. Moreover, the term " God " would then be really something different.

Hence adoptionism is not a fair representation of the implications of faith.

Chalcedon, however, did not remain true to the insights of Nicaea, for it was designed to answer a question that can never be asked, namely, how human and divine natures are related in Christ. To ask the question is to show that one does not understand that only when he experiences the power of the inner life of Jesus can he even speak of God's being there. However, the inner life of Jesus is never effective apart from the man Jesus whose life it was. It is not a question of a divine union with human nature but of the particular importance of one specific Man in history to my salvation.

What is at stake here, Herrmann argues, is the character of salvation. For the Pauline and Johannine view is that salvation is the birth of faith. But another view, which he traces to Irenaeus, involves the restoration of human nature to an incorruptible state by virtue of bestowing upon it the powers of the divine nature. This gives birth to the type of thinking which allows the Chalcedonian formula and permits one to conceive of a hypostatic union. Luther sensed its problem but once again could not find a way beyond Chalcedon and back to Nicaea. The confusion of the later Lutheran doctrine of *communicatio idiomatum* and refinements of this in theories of kenosis is merely testimony to the fact that Luther should have abandoned Chalcedon altogether.[21]

Perhaps we can see here the richness of Herrmann's theological work. He combines the insights of the historian of dogma with systematic rigor. Furthermore, he places himself in the tradition where he found his faith by trying to recapture the basic intention of Luther. But first and foremost he gives expression to faith as it has been given him and in the interest of his students resists the kind of doctrinal woodenness that would destroy for them any possible contact with the religious impulses beginning with Jesus himself.

In this connection the testimony of Herrmann's students begins to make eminent sense. He had about him, they say, an evangelical zeal and warm personal faith. To a generation perplexed by the question of subscription to the Apostles' Creed he was the rallying point for new thought. For many, he was the savior of their faith. It is small wonder that so many paid him tribute, and it is no wonder at all that his ideas permeated so many hideouts of the next generation.

It is my contention that Herrmann's view of the theological task remains correct, but in order to clear the ground for completing this argument, we must survey how the theology that he shaped has been remarkably reshaped.

CHAPTER TWO

The Descendants of Herrmann

To ANYONE VERSED in the theological writings of this century the themes of Herrmann's thought are not foreign. The dissociation of faith from assent to dogma, the raising of questions about the historical Jesus and the dogmatic Christ, the close relationship drawn between religious experience and individual self-realization, and the careful examination of the place of theological language — to name only a few — are common coin. One can even detect in Herrmann's writings a real affinity for Kierkegaard — of which he seemed to be conscious but which he did not pursue.[1] With the fantastic interest in the unhappy Dane, thought that is like his seems very familiar.

Nevertheless, a real watershed stands between Herrmann and us, and even those who wish to revive his thought bring it into contact with quite different problems and with quite different intentions. For since Herrmann wrote, it has become even more commonplace to address oneself to the problems raised by the theology of the Word of God. Chiefly responsible for this, obviously, is Karl Barth.

Barth has been declaimed and defamed. He has been heralded as the founder of a new reformation and looked at in vague disbelief by those who thought the new reformation had already taken place. He has characterized himself and his theology as a footnote and then has gone on to make that footnote a rather lengthy one. He has disavowed the nineteenth century and yet tried valiantly to pay tribute to it. His disciples proclaim that the Barthian era closes forever the era of German liberalism, but the relationship between Barth and his teachers is ambiguous at best. Indisputable is the fact that Barth has left his imprint upon theological work in this century in a remarkable way.

For this reason, it becomes mandatory to see how he took the legacy of his great teacher, Herrmann, and reshaped it. Whether the changes are as dramatic as Barthian apologists claim or whether they are only subtle changes which shift a delicate balance, it is clear, I believe, that Barth left the theological enterprise distinctly transformed. But I wish further to contend that he left it confused and misdirected and that this confusion still reigns.

THEOLOGY AND THE WORD OF GOD

In an early study of Barth's theology which remains to this day extremely valuable, Wilhelm Pauck tried to place him in the context of his generation and ask what really motivated his consistent pursuit of a theology of revelation. Pauck argued that Barth was not alone but part of a larger company of German intellectuals whose world had dissolved and who sought some distinct guideposts from which to pinpoint reality and from which they might gain fundamental orientation. Part of this argument is not unique, for Pauck points out what other interpreters of Barth have done as well. Barth, Thurneysen, and friends were closely identified with the aims of religious socialism and the peace endeavors of socialism throughout Europe. The coming of the war and the failure of the socialists to stand against it fell together with professional problems entailed in the ministry. In order to find an authentic and commanding voice in preaching, they pursued new methods and experienced in attention to Biblical text a living voice.

Pauck argues that rediscovery of a basis for seeing reality once again is not unique to the theology of Barth but only places him in the company of other German intellectuals in the postwar period. Returning from fantastic subjectivism, Pauck claims,

> German man began his recovery. The first sign of his convalescence soon became apparent. The painters ceased to fill the art-galleries with the unproportioned, wildly colored products of a feverish, frantic imagination; the contours of the world as we see it returned and the laws of perspective were no longer violently disobeyed. The subjectivism of their revolutionary art was replaced by what they called a "new objectivism," a "new realism." Soon afterwards the architects inaugurated a new building period by erecting structures of a restrained purposefulness, combining comfort and practical adequacy with simple beauty. The philosophers followed. Phenomenology attempts to overcome the conflicts between objectivism and subjectivism. It aims at a meaningful realism. In every field, there is the beginning of a plan of reconstruction, which observes new laws and rules, described in terms like concreteness, objectivism, factualism, *Sachlichkeit*.[2]

This interesting claim of Pauck's is neither easy to support nor easy to deny, since the German intellectual scene was soon clouded over by Nazism and its legions were dispersed to other lands. However, it has striking implications for the interpretation of Barth's theology, for the generation which followed Barth's lead saw in its entanglement with the church struggle that theological issues were at stake. The Barmen Declaration pitched the choice of resistance or collaboration with the Nazis on a theological note and saw at the root of German Christian nationalism an apostasy from the Word of God.[3] It may well be that the particular political choice taken by the church at this time was not so securely grounded in theology and indeed that a variety of motives actually brought men together in the *Kirchenkampf*.[4]

Now that we can back off from the superheated atmosphere of Nazi Germany and place Barth's initial work in a context like that outlined by Pauck we can see that allegiance to the Word of God is not the only way in which one's world can be reconstructed, nor is it the only defense against national pride gone berserk. And from this point of view we can assess more realistically exactly where Barth's notion of the Word of God came from and what he drew out of it.

It is certainly true as Barth's apologists claim that the problem of the sermon forced him to undertake an examination of his theological presuppositions and to search for a tool that would make the Scriptures come alive for his people. It is also true that the concern he had to make his preaching more than his own pious musings is most admirable. And his arrival at the conviction that only the gracious activity of God touching his words through the words of Biblical text could make them alive is in line with all the emphases of the Pauline gospel.

There should be no wonder that Pauline themes dominate Barth's work and that his entrée into the theological world should come via a large commentary on Romans. Like Augustine and the Reformers, he underscores the claim that without the direct initiative of God man continues to receive the wages of sin. All his endeavors are frustrated by the arrogance of his pride, and all the grandeur of human creativity is subjected to demonic malformation. Every achievement of man must be turned inside out so that its ultimate origin in God may be visible.

The Pauline themes, however, are woven into a symphonic structure that is really more Johannine. The living word of the Bible which speaks through the words of the authors calling in question those who seek to question it has its basis in the Word Incarnate — Jesus Christ the faithful one. Here human sin is judged by being unveiled. Here in one particular man the generalized quest for God — a quest that really masks human pretensions — is scandalized. For here God himself is present, addressing man as his child and reestablishing the relationship that is proper with his creature.

Through his emphasis upon the living word which comes to speech in the words of the preacher and through his focus upon the figure of Christ as Logos incarnate, Barth is able to preserve a theological personalism which was part of his thought from the earliest.[5] God addresses man as a " Thou " in the Word in which he remains " I." [6] And the consequence of this is that a man is called to his proper personhood in knowing God.

By means of his theology of the Word and his focus upon personal life in God and personal response in men Barth makes connection with various classical notions in theology brought together so brilliantly by Augustine.[7] For Logos theology, which affirms that the fundamental principle of creation has been disclosed in the person of Christ and the work that he accomplished, is combined by Augustine with the growing notion of personality in Western thought to form the idea of human freedom in history rooted in the divine life. God, whose personal life is complete in the love of Father for Son and Son for Father, turns *ad extra* to create a world whose perfection is in the man who grows into personal fulfillment by union with the Triune One. This union gives him release from bondage to the material of creation. It gives him freedom in moral purpose and allows him to find his destiny in history. But most important: it gives him knowledge in faith which will finally give way to perfect sight.

In Barth's hands this whole Augustinian pattern is reconstructed. God's self-disclosure in the incarnation is seen to be the only possible genuine manifestation of his trinitarian life. Men and the world receive the clue about their fundamental nature from this union of human and divine in our midst. And we are drawn into true knowledge by the presence of God in the Holy Spirit. The *archē* of creation is revealed in faith.

Here Pauck's analysis of Barth is so pertinent, for the search for the clue to reality which found Barth one among others led him to the classical Christian solution. With him faith as response to the word of God becomes increasingly the means to a knowledge of God which depends upon no particular genius in human culture. To be sure, Barth has always treated faith rather gingerly. In the *Römerbrief,* faith is the point of tangency between God and man — and a point is always without height or breadth. However, in his study of Anselm he became more confident that faith might have some intellectual content and has since testified that this opened up for him the possibilities of writing the *Church Dogmatics*. Even here, nevertheless, faith is always defined by the nature of revelation and it is specifically conditioned by the fact that God's initiative and Lordship are preserved.

Thus Barth's theology is consciously different from Herrmann's. Instead of having faith shape the theological task, it is shaped by revelation by the Word of God rooted in the triune life of God. This, Barth argues, is proper and constitutes the basis of his quarrel with Herrmann. To be sure, he pays tribute to Herrmann for having resisted every attempt to reduce religion to some innate characteristic of men which only needs to be developed. Herrmann really perceived that God is man's Lord and hence protected himself from an attack of the nature of Feuerbach's. Here he stood correctly against Kaftan, Cohen, and Natorp.[8] But he ended in his systematic theology exactly where he should have begun: with the Trinity, the reality of God as God. Hence he only pointed to the true source of religion in the Word of God. Barth confesses that it is really his intention to follow Herrmann's lead by beginning where he ended and ultimately saying everything entirely differently.

However, one must wonder whether indeed Barth does follow out the intention of Herrmann's theology. For his search for the fundamental principle of things — the *archē* of all reality — brings the Christian religion to rather different use. Regardless of the fact that Barth makes much the same use of it as do the classical theologians such as Origen and Augustine — to say nothing of Calvin — this clearly was not the purpose of Herrmann. Faith does not govern the theological enterprise as the essence of Christian experience, but is subservient to revelation. For Barth, this is necessary to prevent an undue subjectivism. But in order to make this judgment he must really misunderstand the real meaning of faith for Herrmann. The latter sees this as the effect of grace upon man which is only preserved in the careful unfolding of the intellectual life as faith coming into speech. To begin with speaking and then come to faith is to destroy the structural connection between them. And this is exactly what Herrmann saw taking place in classical orthodoxy and its shadow, rationalism.

The results in Barth's theology are clearly to be seen. He finds release from the strict limits within which Herrmann had placed the theological enterprise and engages in a vast survey of the intellectual content of revelation. No longer does he feel the restraints of the Kantian critique, and he makes statements laden with metaphysical content if he feels that they are implied in the Word of God. For this he makes no apology.[9] And by such procedure he becomes a classical theologian on the pattern of Calvin or even Thomas. He even rehabilitates dogma as a meaningful theologoumenon shifting its meaning in the light of his theology of the Word so that dogma, like preaching, happens when the Holy Spirit enlivens human words.

Crucial to the distinction between Herrmann and Barth is the interpretation of Christ. Here Barth comes near victory with what he considers to be a mortal wound. He argues that Herrmann's notion of the inner life of Jesus confronting us in the New Testament picture of Christ really rests upon the certainty that God was here in action and not upon any historical encounter with the man Jesus. Herrmann, for whom this was real, had indeed heard the Word of God and proclaimed it — not in the descriptions of Jesus' inner life, but in the powerful claim that God's Word had made upon him. Instead of criticizing the classical Christological dogma, Herrmann should have realized that the New Testament itself really claims the risen and exalted Christ for its authority. Christological orthodoxy merely echoes this claim in more systematic terms. All the actions of the man Jesus gain importance because of the " Beyond " which shines through them.[10]

Now, if I read this argument correctly, it is indeed not insignificant. For classical Christology is not totally out of step with the New Testament in claiming to see the human nature of Jesus of special importance only because of its intimate connection with the divine nature which shines through. Moreover, whether one turns to Mark or John for a picture of Jesus, it is indeed the case that his significance is as a divine epiphany — no matter whether in conflict with demons or in unveiling divine purpose. And no one can overlook in reading Herrmann's works the seeming confidence he had that the New Testament picture of Jesus might communicate in reading and preaching the inner life of this particular man. However, I do not think in the last analysis that Barth's argument is really relevant. Even if we discount the hopes Herrmann had for using the New Testament, we cannot overlook the fact that his argument against Chalcedon pivoted upon the nature of salvation, not upon the question of the historical Jesus. In other words, it was a theological and not a historicocritical argument.

To be sure, Barth also makes it a theological argument — in connection with the doctrine of revelation! But if we take it back into the doctrine of salvation or redemption, it becomes quite clear why Barth can affirm both Chalcedon and its enhypostatic interpretation. For Barth does see human nature transformed in union with divine nature in a way that is quite similar to those in the classical tradition who derive from Irenaeus.[11] And in connection with the redeeming action of God in Christ, faith becomes acknowledgment, recognition, and confession of how the being of man is thereby restored.[12]

For Herrmann, this view of salvation opens the door for a dilution of the Christian religion. Faith becomes knowledge and the assent to dogma. Trust is taken out of the realm of history where personal encounters take place and is related instead to the institution that is the custodian of revelation. And the demand for moral action which is the heartbeat of Christian experience is seriously weakened. In the last analysis the attacks that have lately beset Christians have really been invited.

If one pursues the influence of two-nature Christology upon Barth's theology, he finds that it has an interesting place in the doctrine of revelation also. For here the words of men, whether they are Biblical or in present-day preaching, are drawn into union with God's Word by action of the Holy Spirit. Although there is no denial of the fact that men's words in every era are conditioned by the circumstances that surround them, there is an easy confidence that such conditioning does not present insuperable problems for God and that his self-disclosure in the Word is not hindered. The corruptible may put on the incorruptible in the miraculous action of God.

The implications of this for the theological enterprise are remarkable. For even though one disclaims finality for his theoretical formulations, and even though he may finally discard them, he remains confident in his speaking and writing that the Holy Spirit is bound to the Word of God and will breathe life into those words which witness to it. In this confidence Barth declares theology to be a science which, like all sciences, is determined by its object. The special nature of this determination necessitates certain ideas — such as the *analogia fidei* — but that only makes theology a more exacting science.

In the realm of exegesis two-nature Christology also has its effect. For Barth does not want to deny the historical-critical method which his teachers developed with such acumen. Nor does he remain aloof from following current trends of Biblical scholarship. But these are seen to be distinctly limited disciplines which can never rise beyond the merely human level in dealing with the events of Biblical times. Furthermore, there are important places in which this work is chastened by the knowledge that what is really at stake in this particular set of historical events is God's self-disclosure. Certain conclusions are therefore precluded and certain avenues become fruitful for pursuit. And anyone who has followed Barthian-style exegesis would have to be blind not to see that it is apologetic of a theology of the Word.

This is not the place to raise the question about what style of exegesis may be proper to Herrmann's idea of the historicity of Jesus, but we must notice that it is correlative to his Christology and differs from Barth's as he sees Nicaea differing from Chalcedon. What we must look at now is the way in which Barth's tremendous emphasis upon the Word of God has given shape to the problems that have been considered by his pupils and by his protagonist — Rudolf Bultmann.

WORD AND FAITH

Perhaps more than anyone else Rudolf Bultmann has remained the most loyal disciple of Herrmann. He is fond of quoting Melanchthon through Herrmann that to know God is to know his benefits. He joins thereby with Herrmann in a polemic against metaphysics. For Bultmann, faith also plays an important part in defining the essence of the Christian religion, and faith is seen in connection with the opening of the future and release from bondage to the past. Furthermore, one can see in the whole program of demythologizing the same sort of Kantian outlook that informed Herrmann's thought. Myth and speculation are both attempts to give concrete reality to the transcendent. Both are ruled out by closing the door on questions of first or final causality as this happens in the modern, post-Kantian world.

Nevertheless, Bultmann also stands apart from Herrmann, and his participation together with Barth in the theological battles of the 1920's was no accident. They both subscribed to a theology of the Word. Although Bultmann refused thereby to attach himself to the classical theological tradition in the fashion of Barth, he nevertheless found himself distinguished from the older generation by his sympathetic response to the Pauline notes that Barth had raised.[18] In John also Bultmann heard the address of God in answer to which faith was born and one's world transformed.

This theology of the Word remained with Bultmann long after he refused to break loose with Barth from the Kantian restraints Herrmann had taught them. In fact, it became the vehicle by which he escaped what appeared to be the great dilemma for his master — the problem of the historical Jesus. Instead of seeking for the inner life of Jesus as this was to be seen in the New Testament witness, he pressed on to find the fundamental religious impulse in this particular Jewish eschato-logical prophet. It is to be found, he declares, in the peculiar character of Jesus' preaching whereby the immediacy of God's presence is drawn into connection with the demand that man's proper relationship to God is one of obedience. Against the background of the Judaism of his day Jesus' hearers found themselves revealed in their weakness and potentiality and re-sponded in faith. His speech as word opened the fullness of the present moment to them that its source in God and their des-tiny as men might be seen.[14]

For Bultmann, this possibility of the word and its character in human life fitted in nicely with the things which Barth was saying, with the Protestant predilection for centering the church's life in preaching, and with the historicocritical technique of exploring the Bible not as historical record but as the kerygma of the church. His subsequent research into the problems of New Testament study has been constantly oriented to the ques-tion: How has the kerygma of the church preserved or distorted or merely transformed the initial impulse to faith in Jesus' preaching itself?

From this point of view and from the demands of profes-sional life in studying the New Testament, Bultmann has been loath to follow Barth into the treasure-house of classical the-ology and has not shared Barth's views on exegesis — which appear in direct relationship to his orthodox Trinitarianism and his allegiance to Chalcedonian Christology. Bultmann has al-ways been more perplexed by the problem of the development of theology in early Christianity, and has shown little interest in theology as a constructive science.[15] For this and other rea-sons he has focused upon the present occurrence of the Word and less upon what can be inferred from this about the life of God in himself.

The basic difference between unfolding a theology of the Word in Barth and one in Bultmann has been the source of several major controversies in recent theology. Pupils of both have joined the ranks, and at certain battle cries such as " demythologizing," or " *Heilsgeschichte*," or " the existence of God " have locked in combat. It is beyond my purpose to go in detail into these arguments, for they have the character, in spite of their ferocity, of intramural debates. Presupposed by all is the primacy of the Word in interpreting the nature of the Christian religion, and undiscussed is the question whether faith can indeed be brought into such intimate connection with the Word without doing it some injustice.

Without lining ourselves up in these debates, let us take a brief look at two problems that have been raised as Barthians and Bultmannians have sparred and that belie, it seems to me, some confusion caused by the predominance of the idea of the Word.

Bultmann and his pupils are largely responsible for bringing the problems of history and hermeneutics to our attention. They are related problems, as some have pointed out, having to do with the representation today of things from the past which come to us largely by means of written texts.[16] The touchy nature of these two problems arises from the peculiar formation of our own lives, for as Bultmann has so often pointed out, human life is uniquely historic. It involves a man in the question of his historicity as he knows himself subject to the actions of men and things about him and ponders his place in the flow of time. In the Hebraic-Christian tradition especially the nature of the moral demand presents one with the possibilities of freedom and opens to him the future. This historicity is avoided when we try to lose ourselves in history. The latter is an idea whereby events in time find some unity of meaning which in effect closes the future and submerges freedom. The gospel, however, calls one back to his historicity.

Furthermore, as Ebeling is fond of reiterating, human life is peculiar by virtue of man's linguisticality. Speech is part and parcel of self-realization, personal interaction, understanding, moral insight and action, and all the various things that we often call human dignity. Moreover, speech cannot be reduced to the means by which all these things are brought about. It is too integrally connected with them and not just the way internal things are externalized.

Thus to interpret written documents in such a way that the historicity of other men is adequately considered involves the kind of participation by the interpreter that is of necessity subjective. Bultmann's dictum here is that the greatest subjectivity is the greatest objectivity. In relationship to the New Testament, if Bultmann's thesis of the kerygmatic center of New Testament religion is correct, the problem of history and the problem of hermeneutics are further complicated. For what is at stake is the declaration to each interpreter of his own historicity. If he is not aware of this, then he is bound to misinterpret the text. However, in finding that the New Testament text really calls him in question, one is raised to the full potentiality of his existence by realizing his linguisticality. A word event takes place which is in essence the basic experience of the Christian religion. The hermeneutical task is then in fact the theological task. For here faith comes to speech.

All of this rests upon certain rather tenuous connections. First of all, even if we should allow that Jesus' initial religious impulse did arise from the character of his preaching and the response it evoked from his listeners, and even if we acknowledge that this was a word event, that is no reason to infer that primitive Christian religion is essentially kerygmatic. But if we should follow along and acknowledge that Pauline and Johannine Christianity is intelligible only in the light of the kerygmatic activity of the church, this does not allow us to draw the further conclusion that preaching the Word has thus been attached forever to the religious impulses deriving from Jesus. Surely preaching has not always in the church been kerygma, and surely there have been times when the Christian religion lived without much real connection with preaching and relied upon liturgical or other activities. Examination of the early church would seem to indicate that Jesus was seen to exercise power in ways that can be called " word event " only by the wildest stretch of the imagination. In fact, I fear that I detect a Protestant bias here which is not wholly acknowledged and which has gained its influence in the present century through powerful representatives of a theology of the Word.

Next we must notice that two particular intellectual activities have been drawn together which need not be so closely related. The one involves coming to terms with the heritage of the Christian religion as this is especially reflected in verbal expressions from the past. The nature of this task must concern us a great deal more, but it must be noted now that this is closely connected with the present form which this religion takes. The other activity is the attempt to analyze the general historical and hermeneutical problems that any humanist faces and which are extremely relevant for one who looks at the Christian tradition. To be sure, these two activities are not totally unrelated. Coming to terms with one's heritage involves in this day and age the use of historical, critical, and hermeneutical techniques which are adequate. However, the relationship between these two activities has been prejudged by the theology of the Word of God by seeing kerygmatic action at the heart of the Christian religion. Verbal expressions past and present are connected by the fundamental impulses that derive from Jesus, and the problems of history and hermeneutics are therefore elevated to become the chief theological problems. With this elevation they are drawn away from the sphere of the humanist in such a way that he often fails to understand their use.

Now, I mean not to overlook the intimate connection between the Christian and the humanistic traditions and I mean to explore the importance of Christian religious impulses for the growth of historical consciousness. But in order to see whether these two distinct intellectual activities might have a much more subtle connection, such exploration must be undertaken without commitment to a theology of the Word. Only then will one see the difficulty of the theological task.

An attack on a theology of the Word runs the risk of calling in question the whole Protestant enterprise. This is especially true since Barth, Bultmann, and their followers have seen their work as a recovery of those impulses which are at the heart of the Reformation. They find their return to the Word and its Biblical source in tune with Luther's rediscovery of the gospel in the Scriptures. Furthermore, they are sensitive to the subtleties of Luther's exegetical methods and his desire to emphasize the living Word which redeems in calling one to faith.

Nevertheless, the one who attacks a theology of the Word need not thereby declare himself apart from or even alienated from the Reformation tradition. In fact, Herrmann was adamant in claiming to represent this tradition and the part Luther played in beginning it. All that is raised by criticism of the prevailing tendency in much of modern theology — interestingly enough in the descendants of Herrmann — is the question about what is indeed at stake in the Reformation and how it relates to our own course in present-day religious life.

This question is all the more pertinent since present-day theologies of the Word as opposed to Luther's are informed by notions that derive from German Idealism and give them a distinctly idealistic cast. It is no accident that Bultmann and his disciples find fellow travelers in the followers of Heidegger. Here the close relationship between reality, idea, and speech is affirmed. Furthermore, it is a matter of record that classical Augustinian theology is full of Platonic assumptions and draws great strength from Neoplatonist idealism. Faith as response to the Word has a heavy content of gnosis — much more so than in Herrmann.

All these contentions must be further explicated and will be in the course of other chapters. They can be drawn roughly together at this point by saying that for me the notion of the Word of God becomes increasingly suspect. Furthermore, it is a notion that is entirely foreign to Herrmann's thought and represents a significant change in emphasis in doing theology which has serious consequences. These consequences are not necessarily the ones which Barth insists upon — that the priority and freedom of God are protected. They are rather, it seems to me, a reinstatement of the trend toward seeing faith as illumination and insight, no matter whether this is an insight into the nature of reality or an understanding of existence. Herrmann's careful connecting of faith and moral action is short-circuited in this process.

For example, Herrmann was fond of criticizing Lutheran orthodoxy for separating faith into three moments — *notitia, assensus,* and *fiducia.* Such a separation is fatal to faith, since *notitia* and *fiducia* should be kept carefully together in order to explicate how one in confrontation with men of faith is called to faithful life himself. Although there is no attempt — with the exception of Pannenberg — to go back to these classical distinctions in the present day, *notitia* dominates *fiducia* to the point that the latter becomes rather a personalizing or " existen-tializing " of knowledge in faith.

To keep proper balance in the conception of faith, then, necessitates an examination of the adequacy of the Word as a means for interpreting the Christian religion and retaining the vitality of the Christian gospel. The bulk of this essay will include such an examination. Before proceeding to this job, however, we must pause to see how the theology of the Word has confused certain of the controversies in recent theology.

JESUS AND REVELATION

The so-called " new quest for the historical Jesus " is the interesting result of scholarly research pushing behind the kerygmatic picture of Jesus the Christ in the New Testament to that in the character of Jesus himself which gave initial impulse to the Christian religion. It differs from the old quest in its awareness that no discovery is going to be made of Jesus' religious life which can be the basis of religious inspiration today. Rather, it begins with the kerygmatic demand of the New Testament that one lift the burden of his existence and be drawn into life in the new aeon of grace and move back behind this kerygma to the man whose own understanding of existence originated it. This is not an attempt to avoid the burden of faith, for it is exactly in faith that the person of Jesus is comprehensible. Furthermore, one comes to appreciate that the New Testament kerygma was in fact the only way in which the real significance of Jesus as a historical person could be preserved. Robinson calls this the New Testament's " historiography."

This " historiography " in the New Testament is analogous to the historiography of the modern day in which one is ready to ask the intention of an author from the past and to see in his representation of things his own understanding of existence. In fact, modern historiography enhances one's ability to come to terms with the New Testament portrayal of Jesus as the Christ. " It is because modern historiography mediates an existential encounter with Jesus, an encounter also mediated by the *kerygma,* that modern historiography is of great importance to Christian faith." [17]

The new quest for the historical Jesus has as its intent " to arrive at an understanding of Jesus' historical action and existential selfhood, in terms which can be compared with the *kerygma.*" [18] This is accomplished by meeting the person Jesus in his sayings and actions in which his " intention and selfhood are latent." [19] What distinguishes this quest from the proclamation of the early church is its desire to separate Jesus from kerygma, not because they are antithetical but because they are different points on the time scale of Christian development. Thus one is engaged in a historical exercise and makes use of historical-critical tools.

Now, at first glance this bears real resemblance to what Herrmann has to say about the problem of the historical Jesus. The historian has to take seriously the fact that the Christian religion claims to be derived from Jesus and to receive its basic impulses from him. To neglect this fact is to preclude in any way understanding Christianity on its own terms. The new quest, at least within the prescription Robinson gives for it, tries to follow out this Herrmannian insight.

The real problem comes up when one reflects upon Herrmann's remarkable assertion that Jesus' inner life as his consciousness always remains his secret. One only knows this inner life as it is mediated by the church and therefore as the inner life of those who now have faith. For inner life — and therefore what Herrmann means by historical life — is found only in the tension of the present when the past loses its hold and one faces the future in freedom. To know history for Herrmann is to make it. Historical understanding in the sense of historiography would bear a relationship to the knowledge of history that psychology bears to ethics.

From this point of view it becomes apparent that the new quest is not really new except in its sophisticated techniques for opening up the development of Biblical religion. And indeed these are extremely valuable. However, the theological justification for attempting the new quest rests upon the assumption that kerygmatic theology is proper theology and that the Christian religion is essentially word event.

The curious figure in the whole debate which surrounds the new quest is Bultmann himself, who is somehow conscious that he has fathered an illegitimate child. Joining with certain critics of Robinson, he notes that the question of historical continuity between Jesus and the kerygma of the church is not really the same question as the material continuity between the religious event which took place when Jesus preached and the religion which is found about the kerygma of the church.[20] Whereas one as historian might probe behind the kerygmatic representation of Jesus as the one in whom the decisive eschatological event has taken place to a man who as a Jew may have stepped outside Judaism's bounds, he must be aware as theologian that the kerygma necessitates an experience of eschatological immediacy. By definition this is not an experience of historical understanding coming from historical research, even though, if we may put it this way, it makes possible real experience of history.

By insisting upon the eschatological aspect of the kerygma, Bultmann reaffirms what Herrmann spoke of as the secret of Jesus forever inaccessible to historical understanding. What he does *not* do is go on to ask whether kerygma, preaching, Word, are proper notions for retaining within faith the eschatological tension or whether they with their counterparts — self-understanding or understanding of existence — do not invite connections with understanding and knowledge in other forms. Is not an idealist slip showing? It would seem so, and this would seem to account for the adoption of a view of history in which the idealist themes — seen from Hegel to Collingwood — predominate.[21]

To be sure, we are confronted here with a difficulty of which Herrmann was not fully enough aware. For the eschatological tension so necessary for the preservation of faith arises from the death of Jesus and the place this death has in the shape of the Christian religion. Faith in Christ is faith in the resurrected one in whom the end has come and the old aeon closed. Herrmann rather easily interpreted the death of Jesus in the Synoptic terms of obedience to his calling. This is seen reflected in the obedience of faith in which one shoulders his own cross and accepts the burdens of moral life in history. Sensitivity to the New Testament gospel of the resurrected One with all its eschatological overtones is surely lacking. Moreover, the figure of the obedient Christ is open to some real question in the light of modern research.

All this is not to say, however, that kerygmatic theology is the proper way to do justice to the eschatological tension which is so integral to the Christian religion. In fact, I shall try later to argue that Herrmann's basic ideas can be altered to take account of the more recent problems in New Testament criticism surrounding the death and resurrection of Jesus. Recourse to a theology of the Word is not necessarily the answer, although I will concede that it is an attractive alternative by virtue of the nature of human speaking and hearing. The furtive quality of speech, the immediacy of communication in verbal exchanges, the many psychological and noetic dimensions which are to be seen in conversation, and many other things contribute to making the word a most available key to human experience in history. It seems to take most adequate account of the unique quality of life in the present in expectation of the future and in separation from the past.

One could argue as I have neither the space nor inclination to do here that kerygmatic theology or theologies of the Word have made rather uncritical and poetic use of the phenomenon of human speech and cannot be taken seriously for this reason. I wish only to conclude that they bring the idea of faith into such company that it loses the precise and theologically significant place it had in Herrmann's thought. Furthermore, in their wake they bring problems that for Herrmann had ceased to have such magnitude and could be adequately dealt with. In the form they take with a theology of the Word, however, they can bring one back into the very kind of theological world that Herrmann wished to avoid.

It is in this world that a rather recent entrant upon the theological scene lives. Wolfhart Pannenberg, a young German theologian who pays tribute to his study under Gerhard von Rad and speaks authoritatively in certain Lutheran circles, also is a critic of theologies of the Word. He is seen in opposition to the disciples of Bultmann and has been in *Auseinandersetzung* with Gerhard Ebeling. Pannenberg is quite at home with the theology of the Lutheran scholastics and is not embarrassed to take up the questions they argued. In this vein he makes the unabashed claim that faith is based upon a knowledge that comes from encounter with the history of Jesus Christ, incarnate Son, risen now in glory.

Pannenberg seems to me to be arguing that theologies of the Word have tendencies toward gnosticism and Pelagianism which are fatal to the gospel.[22] For the understanding of existence that comes in encounter with the kerygma is not just the understanding one would have who reads the New Testament correctly. It involves personal decision of a particular kind and hence may really be seen as a new supernaturalism. In Barthian theology and in a Lutheran such as Althaus the special nature of this experience is accounted for by reference to the Holy

Spirit, but this merely goes counter to the intention of the New Testament — shared by the Reformers [23] — that the gospel is clear to those who will just listen. Blindness and stubbornness and closed ears can only be called unwillingness to understand. The action of the Spirit in understanding is not supernatural but rather is the most natural thing possible.

In line with this claim — which seems hard to refute on historical grounds alone — Pannenberg goes on to insist that when one faces the problem of revelation he cannot avoid a particular sequence of ideas that is quite reasonably drawn from the set of events which culminate in Jesus' resurrection. What one means by God and divinity must be specific but must also have claim upon all men. This happens when human history is seen as the stage upon which the actions of God are clearly to be observed. The particular circumstances of Israelite history provide this stage, and by virtue of the crises in Israelite life, caused by the destruction of Jerusalem resulting in the rise of apocalyptic, connection is made with the Greek search for the God who comprehends all reality. The meaning in history is disclosed only at the end of history and therefore every particular history points beyond itself. However, in Jesus Christ the truth of the end of history has been made manifest as he was " raised from the dead." [24]

This raising of Jesus requires careful treatment, since all speech about the end of history must be metaphorical. Thus descriptions of the risen Lord always point beyond themselves to a new reality with which our present life provides only weak analogies. However, like the Greek notion of immortality for the soul, they speak to that dimension of human life which may be called openness for the world. I take this to mean that one without losing his finite existence and its boundaries knows some participation in that which is infinite. He does so by seeing in the resurrection the fundamental clue to universal history in which he himself is included: that the idea of history itself is his participation in the infinite or his union with God.[25]

Ingenious as this may be, it is really Hegel stood on his

head. One does not transcend finitude by dialectical understanding, for that in effect freezes the future and closes it. But one remains in history questioned by history in the light of the transcendence of the end of history. I must admit that at this point I do not know whether this means that the ideal is the real or the real the ideal or whether neither applies. At any rate, faith has become illumination and revelation has become particular events in human history which as the object of faith provide this illumination. Faith is trust in this knowledge of the meaning of life. It is one with hope in the future resurrection of all.

In all of this, one has the strange feeling that everything being said is very plausible and that a certain air of mystery surrounding the work of the post-Bultmannians is dispelled. At the same time it is apparent that a remarkable credulity is elicited from the reader. He is even asked to trust the accounts of physical resurrection. Moreover, the whole of human culture by being given a center is now encompassed in an ever more widening circle. What we now have is a new synthesis of faith and knowledge which takes stock of the necessity to include not only natural occurrences but historical process. It is, in Herrmann's terms, a *Religionsphilosophie,* even though it has important predecessors in the history of theology.

I wonder if anyone other than the servants of confessionalism would take Pannenberg seriously had not the work of Barth, Bultmann, and others through theologies of the Word brought faith back into intimate connection with knowledge. Without the problems of hermeneutics and history would there be a place for one to assert again a comprehensive theological scheme like this? Is it not the restoration of a particular view of revelation which lays the groundwork for Pannenberg's ruminations? To be sure, Herrmann deals with revelation but allows it only in the experience of being redeemed. This is the same experience in which we find ourselves called to faith and moral action. Thus Herrmann puts limits around the idea of revelation that restrict its theological use. These limits are broken by the idea of the Word and confusion is introduced. Only with this confusion is it possible for Pannenberg to raise the points he does.

WHEN TO SPEAK THEOLOGICALLY?

The interesting thing about Pannenberg is that his historical observations are often extremely illuminating and bring to light positions held by Christian writers that run quite counter to those who claim to be their descendants.[26] However, these observations do not seem to me to be theologically relevant. For to prove that Luther may indeed not have thought what Gogarten thinks, or that Paul did indeed have an experience of a bodily risen Lord, or that Luke-Acts represents a healthy balance to gnosticizing tendencies in Paul and John may say absolutely nothing theologically. And here we come to the heart of the matter. For Herrmann really sensed the limits within which theology moves and saw that although it bordered on historical thinking, it had a distinct place of its own.

The question as to what might properly constitute theology and when one might be said to be speaking theologically has been confused by recent trends. Barth is, I believe, the one who began these trends and even his critics in the past few years are more deeply indebted to him than they might think. The result has been that classical theological problems and the philosophical issues entailed in them have been reintroduced into contemporary theological discussion without the proper assessment as to whether they are appropriate.

I must confess that, for all its attractiveness, the neoclassical philosophical theology espoused by Schubert M. Ogden on the basis of the work of Charles Hartshorne falls in this category. Not just the label " neoclassical " identifies it with traditional issues from past centuries. The whole enterprise that finds one of its points of origin in the speculations of Whitehead repeats the philosophical attempt to extrapolate on the scientific picture of the world which is now current in order to root cosmological theory in metaphysical doctrines. I leave to the philosopher the judgment as to whether this is fruitful philosophical work. That it belongs to the realm of theology as Herrmann saw this is definitely open to question.

It is certain, however, that many theologians today find this procedure quite in order. But they are either the ones who have been seduced by Barth's theology of the Word to consider faith in connection with knowledge and revelation or they are the ones who have always taken an apologetic stance against the challenges modern men have raised to faith. Herrmann as defender of faith had penetrated directly to the question: What really can be correctly said to be theology, and where does one now find it responsibly exercised?

In the light of the present confusion or disagreement about what might be proper to theology, Herrmann's case must be more thoroughly outlined. This must be done with reference to the life of faith in Christian history, for it is here that the theological task has received its shape.

CHAPTER THREE

The Shape of Orthodoxy

A PERSPECTIVE IS GIVEN on the important reshaping of the theological task by theologies of the Word when one reflects on Herrmann's critique of orthodoxy. He asserted emphatically the independence of faith from the demand for subscription to creeds, finding it injurious to faith itself. Although no rebirth of rigid creedalism is evident in recent theology, the sharpness of Herrmann's distinction has been reduced. Outlining the basis for this distinction is the task of this chapter, and further pursuing its consequences leads to definite insights about theology itself.

The task set is complicated by the fact that one must seek to recapture the ground on which Herrmann's argument is built without raising on this ground the same structure. Herrmann not only made claims for the New Testament picture of Jesus which are now suspect; he also labeled classical orthodoxy Roman Catholicism and charged to its account the development of creedalism. To be sure, he saw a reconstruction of Catholicism on Protestant soil, but his argument has a flavor to it that should cause some distaste to one today apprised of the complex nature of Protestantism and conscious of how blurred the lines between the Roman and other traditions have become.

For our purposes, it appears more significant and accurate to speak of the shaping of an orthodox view of faith which took place in the history of faith and then to look at the reshaping of faith and the corresponding theological task in and following the Reformation. The fundamental outlines of Herrmann's case will be retained but the content will be somewhat changed.

It is important to insist upon indebtedness to Herrmann, since the legacy of orthodoxy is considerable and the work of recent theologians has tended to obscure the clear separation he made between faith and the affirmation of doctrine. Thus in the popular mind and in certain circles of technical theology there is still the tendency to bring faith into too close connection with statements of belief no matter how well guarded these statements may be. And no matter how sophisticated the disclaimers and qualifications that surround " statements of faith " may be, their very existence provides the occasion for skeptical reaction, cynical analysis, or just quizzical mystification on the part of many educated men.

From the outset let it also be clear that the pages which follow are not just an exercise in historical analysis. Not only are they too brief and sketchy for that, but they are not intended to provide a full picture of the body of Christian doctrine, its history and development. I do not wish to reflect on the intricacies of church history. It is a theological point that is to be made by reflecting upon the history of faith. Theology, as we shall see, comes into being in specific circumstances and for specific reasons. If it is Christian theology according to the notion of Chistianity found in Herrmann, then it is related to faith and its communication. No treatment of it is adequate unless some reference to the concrete communication of faith is constantly maintained.

Clarity on this matter will help us avoid a simple but persistent mistake which often besets theological reflection. This is that the primitive events of Christian history have a clear unity to them and in this unity is the authentic impulse of the Christian religion. Appeal to apostolic times or to Peter, Paul, or the Synoptic tradition is supposed to establish the authority of what is being claimed. This appeal, however, must run counter to the conclusions of those who do research on Christian origins.[1] The complexity of Jewish religion in the Hellenistic world and the ambiguous place of early Christian communities in it is now seen to be great indeed. Even the historian seeks some tools of organization whereby a sense of unity can be brought to the very diverse phenomena uncovered.

We could proceed to argue that all historical analysis is beset with decisions of value and importance which arise from the particular existence of the researcher. Nothing as extensive as this is necessary now, however, for I wish to pursue a clearly Herrmannian line in assessing the development of theology and use for this purpose a process of selection determined to be fair to historical materials but designed also to look at the Christian religion from the perspective of faith as Herrmann conceived this.

From the beginning we can call this a form of Paulinism for reasons that will become apparent. This should not surprise us unless we incorrectly feel that the " crisis theologians " alone returned to Pauline insights. Herrmann consciously sought to follow Luther and in the process echoed distinctly Pauline themes. Although it may seem odd at first to claim that an attack on orthodoxy might arise from Paul, this is exactly what I wish to argue, for in this way aspects of the notion of faith can be isolated for treatment which both indicates the direction that orthodoxy took that was in certain measure legitimate and also provides the critical tools for disengaging from orthodoxy in a new setting. It should be no secret that such disengagement is presently the order of the day.

FAITH AS LIFE IN THE NEW AGE AND THE JOHANNINE PROVENANCE

In order immediately to take stock of Herrmann's overconfidence in the power of the Biblical picture of Jesus to arouse faith, we must acknowledge that now this Biblical picture is seen to be the kerygmatic witness of writers in the early church shaped by postresurrection reflections and the particular problems of first-century Christians. Even though Herrmann was

anything but naïve about the New Testament presentation of
Jesus, he was not as thoroughly aware as we are today of the
far-reaching influence of first-century concerns.

He did, however, provide a way for viewing the documents
of the New Testament which is anything but out of date. For
he emphasized that the heart of Jesus' inner life — his own relationship with God — was his own secret forever. If we pursue this notion, we shall arrive, I believe, at the conclusion that
every attempt to find in the figure of Jesus in the New Testament an example or an epitome of faith is not only bound to
fail but is mistaken in intention. It is psychologizing whether
its techniques are that of the old or the new quest for Jesus'
historical character.

The proper question to ask of the New Testament is how the
religious tradition that Jesus founded came to identify faith so
closely with the religious impulse it bore. Why did the complex
of words associated with *pistis* and its Hebrew predecessors
seem proper for describing the new life which they felt to be
upon them when Jesus was seen to have accomplished messianic work? These words, of course, all have the basic intention of expressing trust in something which is reliable.[2] They
are not the only words used by the early Christians, but they
came to have in the Pauline and Johannine literature crucial
significance. Through them the whole of Christian history came
to see faith as of prime importance.

Faith is suggestive for the interpretation of Christian experience because it seems to come most to terms with the impact
of Jesus' preaching and the nature of his Messiahship. It was
the peculiar originality of Jesus in the context of Palestinian
Judaism where eschatological expectations ran high to bring
the immediacy of God's rule in the future into connection with
the prophetic demand for obedience to God's will. His place
either as Messiah or as herald of the Messianic Age was hinged
to his success in bringing those Jews who heard him to a sense
of the pregnancy of the present moment which might even now
give birth to the new age. Such a sense brought with it a shap-

ing of one's life in line with the divine demands.[3]

Jesus' messianic role in ushering in the new age is fixed in the traditions of the church by the experience of the resurrection — whatever that may have been.[4] Now the end is upon us and the church lives in expectation of its full culmination. And it is this life in expectation which is characterized by faith. In Pauline terms it is also the age of the spirit; our justification is now to be found in the new life of the resurrected Christ. This is a life of freedom in which one may come to true obedience to the will of God unencumbered by the power of sin and death.

Paul was conscious that this life of faith involved trials which tested its character as trust. Relying on God in the times of the Messianic Age included rejoicing in one's sufferings as the woes of this age beset the faithful. As a preacher Paul saw his mission as announcing to all men the closing of the old aeon and the opening of the new in the cross of Christ.

Faith in his listeners was not so much trust in the reliability of his message as trust in the power of Christ now exercised over sin and death to overcome the ultimate power of evil forces.[5] It shapes the life one lives and is active in love. Here it parallels the structure of the new life men were called to in hearing from Jesus' own lips the announcement of the imminent coming of the Kingdom and the demand for obedience to the will of God.[6] As hope this new life included confident entry into the future.

In the Johannine school, faith is seen more as trust in the message of the church issuing forth in a new life of love toward the brethren. It is drawn into connection with the picture of Jesus as the Word Incarnate. Thus does the trust of the man of faith seem to be anchored in the disclosure by Jesus' preaching and action of a secret hidden from ordinary men. To those, however, who now hear his word — presumably in the words of contemporary preachers and writers — true knowledge comes and leads to new life. To be sure, this knowledge involves illumination in new birth and the power of the Spirit, but it is more closely related to a community that bears definitive revelation than with a community that finds its life determined by the woes of the Messianic Age.

Whether the Johannine picture of Jesus and faith reflects a later period when eschatological expectations had to be revised to deal with a delayed Parousia, or whether it merely represents a variation in interpreting the significance of Jesus as Christ need not bother us. Such a critical question does not hide the fact that two different emphases are seen in the Pauline and Johannine schools when the idea of faith is at issue. In a sense one can say that Herrmann's quarrel with orthodoxy goes back to this difference. For he wishes to see faith as characteristic of the life one is called to in the new age rather than as a response to revelation — even though this be rooted in the figure of Jesus himself — leading to true knowledge. And he is resisting, I believe, a tendency that has manifested itself throughout Christian history to read Paul through the gospel of John and give too much prominence to faith as response to the Word.

This tendency to read Paul through the eyes of John is consistent with the Johannine provenance. For it incorporates the various parts of early church tradition into a consistent set of ideas which form the content of knowledge coming from revelation. The power of this tendency can be seen in very many ways, but it becomes especially strong, as we shall observe, when in the third and fourth centuries a theology of illumination grows up.

Remarkable indeed has been the power of this Johannine tendency to influence our conceptions of how the religious impulses originating from Jesus have been passed along. One consciously or unconsciously overlooks the fact — especially if he is Protestant — that disposition toward life consistent with the obedience Jesus demanded of his listeners or with Pauline faith can arise in a variety of ways. The part played by spoken words or verbalization is a thing to be discovered and one dare not assume that the Johannine account of this part is definitive for Christian history.

When this has been clearly recognized, one must then ask what structures arose within the Christian community to keep faith — now interpreted in a Herrmannian way in dependence upon Paul — alive. And the place of verbal expression in these structures must be assessed. This, I would take it, is the implication of form-critical techniques, and what is rather surprising is that it has not been pursued by theologians more fully.[7]

Perhaps most neglected by Protestant theologians but now increasingly in the forefront of Roman Catholic thought is the reassessment of the function of liturgical life. With renewed emphasis upon the liturgy as rehearsal of the eschatological mysteries within the community of faith as one waits for the culmination of Christ's victory over the present age, we can come to appreciate the complex connection of word, action, emotion, *esprit de corps,* and so forth, which might induce in a man the kind of trust and confidence that are integral to faith. Words in this context may be rhetorical in importance. They may carry meaning in strange proportion to their ability to illumine reality. And they may indeed merely measure the rhythm of the common life.

The attempts that are numerous in every period of church history to regulate the life of faith and to define the character of its novelty form structures that are also of importance in shaping men's dispositions. And although the Protestant theologian is prone to run up the red flag of law when reflecting upon church discipline and the traditional morality which it produces, the fact remains that faith may be either nurtured or destroyed thereby, depending upon the quality of life resulting. In their favor we may enter that the moral traditions and institutions of the church have contained a large dose of eschatological expectancy consistent with Pauline faith. The life of the Christian over against the world is defined by the battle of the new age to overcome the old. The rigorous discipline of the monk, for example, is a witness to the eschatological gospel the church bears and brings one up against the impact of God's

Kingdom in the present moment concretely and dramatically. Moreover, religious exercises as they later grew up within distinct communities of faith are directed — if they are genuine to faith — toward the culmination of the great struggle of Christ with the powers of darkness.

To bring to attention the place of liturgy, discipline, and additional things such as church order and insist that they are important in shaping the life of faith in the Christian community is to raise some rather interesting questions. For example, one must examine with great care the relationship between Christian communities and their counterparts in Judaism. And when one is dealing with liturgy and discipline, it becomes readily apparent that the religious impulses which derive from Jesus are closely intertwined with the Jewish traditions in which he was involved. But more significant for the theological task is the question of what language current in the church in a particular period can actually be called theological. Are the creedal formulations detected by certain critics in New Testament materials and seen later on in the baptismal creeds of the organized church to be read for their philosophical content or as a mixture of interpretative, institutional, and hymnic language? Are standards of judgment applied to men's actions derived from some sort of reflection about the correct way to state the significance of Jesus or rather from concern with particular implications of these actions within the community and its history? Can one take liturgical expressions out of their liturgical context — as is done even in the New Testament — without changing their meaning and importance?

Of course, answers to questions like these are extremely difficult to come by and require in many cases a prior judgment about the real nature of the Christian religion and what is essential to it. From the perspective of Herrmann one would have to say, I think, that all words and actions which carry along and bring one in contact with the inner life of Jesus — or to faith — must be understood by the theologian in relation to this function. They may be examined historically in this way and may also be judged as to their adequacy or inadequacy accordingly. But the content and philosophical implications of expressions within the church become " statements of faith " only when one has followed the Johannine provenance and started down the path to classical orthodoxy.

The interesting result of following this Herrmannian line of interpretation is that it calls to our attention the fact that it is historically inappropriate to speak of theology in the Christian church until well after the period of the New Testament. And to speak of Christian theology is to presuppose the remarkable combination of the content of the church's gospel and the ideals of the Greek philosophers which occurs in the second century and finds its brilliant example finally in the Alexandrians Clement and Origen. Before this time there are precursors for theology in the development of the church's teaching office and the attempt to find the fulfillment of the Hebrew Scriptures in Jesus. And for this purpose the methods and traditions of Jewish scribes are used and adopted by the church. To call this theology in the original sense of the word,[8] however, is to attribute to it a function within the life of the community that neither its thought patterns nor means of expression seem to justify. Rather, one has to see here a way of justifying Christian claims about Jesus' Messiahship and his place within the promises and hopes of Israel. The intention does not seem to be to illumine one about the nature of God, man, and the world, but to bring one into the orbit of the church as a citizen of the messianic community.

Of course, questions arise in this sort of enterprise which may later be seen to have theological implications. Furthermore, speculation about things such as law, wisdom, the Messiah, and the like in Judaism had given rise to a schematization — often in dependence upon mythological means of expression — of orders and powers in the cosmos that were eventually drawn into theological understanding. Almost from the beginning of the church Jesus is related to these schemes and his place in them is explained. But it nevertheless takes the translation of schematizations like this into the world of the philosophical schools before one has theology in the full sense of the word.[9]

When this happens a merging of diverse ideas results. In the first place, one asserts that a traditional set of expressions, images, and procedures for action — either as contained in sacred written sources or in the teachings that surround them — actually is the key for understanding the world and one's place in it. To this is added that such an understanding brings insight into the reality of all things in this world. Furthermore, by this insight the proper nature of human mental activities is brought out and hence anyone who thinks will respond to these traditional images favorably. Finally, by means of the various aspects of this tradition human life and culture may be perfected.

To explain the power of this amalgam of ideas and its influence on Western culture is beyond us now, but to indicate how faith as trust in the power of the new age inaugurated by the Christ passes over into the response to a tradition represented theologically must detain us for a while.

THE RELIGIOUS AND INTELLECTUAL NOTIONS OF ILLUMINATION

For Herrmann, nothing was so important to the life of faith as the sense of freedom that made moral life a possibility. To live in this freedom is, it seems to me, of the same order as living in the new age inaugurated by the messianic work of Jesus. It is also to be found in the piety of the church in the first few centuries where men are conscious of being brought into a new freedom from the evils of the pagan world and the hope of sharing in divine perfection. To be sure, there are remarkable differences that indicate interesting cultural developments, but the adaptation of the ideals produced by the best in Greek culture which took place in the Christian church and their transformation into a new humanism [10] cannot help being looked upon with favor by one interested in restating Herr-mann's case.

Here the Stoic notions of transcending passion and involve-ment in necessity are transformed into a Christian ideal of *apatheia* brought about by the discipline of the church. Christ, the instructor, whose words are heard in the whole moral tradi-tion of Jewish and Christian history leads one to the sort of self-possession that saves him not only from the foolish reli-gions of the pagans but from the sort of attachment to life in this world which will make death an ultimate threat to him.

Such freedom is of a piece with the proper place of man in created order. Thus his enslavement to the passions is not au-thentic to his nature but the result of foolish misuse of freedom that ends in his being blinded to his possibilities and in his losing the vision of the truth that might set him at one with reality. To correct this error and to restore man in freedom God has disclosed the truth in the incarnation of the Logos. Thus Christ as instructor not only guides one into those paths of life where he is free but also bestows again the vision of truth which allows him to understand the world and his place in it.

Thus the philosophical interest is allied with the interest in moral instruction — as perhaps it always should be. The apol-ogists began the attempt to work out this synthesis of ideas which consummated the wedding between Hebraic–Christian religious consciousness and the aims of Hellenic culture em-bodied in the institution of education. Christians made use of the existing schools and integrated the legacy of Greece with the traditions of Jews and Christians. This is brilliantly ex-emplified in the Alexandrians and is continued in the classical theology of third, fourth, and fifth centuries. Here the purpose of education was seen to be a perfecting of the freedom one came to in faith whereby one understood the work of the Logos to stand both at the fountainhead of creation and behind the Scriptural tradition of the church. Philosophical speculation was merely the elucidation of why one knew redemption in the activities of the Christ, but it was that proper love of wisdom found in the man who was becoming like God.

In this context the Scriptures functioned as the custodian of the mysteries that are disclosed by the Logos to that one who by his faith has been opened to them.[11] Thus to have proper understanding of them and proceed beyond the level of the literal text to the spiritual meaning latent in them required a further perfecting of man involved. He as the Gnostic is able to lead the community in the life of faith.

Knowledge is the result of illumination. The mind that had been blind in the darkness is filled with light, and with light comes clarity. Thus philosophy when properly done is an exercise of the mind that shares in the light. The integration of faith and reason in Christian theology plays heavily upon the idea of enlightenment or illumination and attributes this to the action of God from whom all light comes.

At this point we must notice how closely interconnected are the religious experiences of redemption and freedom with the theological enterprise. For light and darkness are important themes in religious expression relating perhaps to the deepest human fears and the most basic human drives for existence and health. To be translated out of darkness into light is to be brought out of death and into life. And it is no accident that these themes play such an important role in religious life in the Hellenistic world interwoven with a man's sense of bondage or freedom.

In the Christian tradition these themes are introduced into liturgy and song, into exhortation and explanation, to show how potent the activity of the Christ is seen to be and how fundamental the significance of his activity on earth. As in Judaism, the eschatological age is understood as the age of light, and the life of the Christian in this new age is conceived of as his illumination.

In particular, by the beginning of the third century when the cult of the sun had assumed importance in the Roman Empire, the Christian rhetorician could contrast the true source of light with the sun and actually demonstrate — at least to his satisfaction — that from this source comes true illumination. In the same way certain cultic acts in Christendom shared the use of sun imagery. The Lord's Day was Sunday, and the rising of the sun was seen to symbolize the rising of Christ from the grave at the resurrection, defeating forever the powers of darkness. But here the sun was merely an *eikōn* of the true light that illumines the world. It is a concrete example of the more general illumination spoken of by the theologians.[12]

No one can really come to terms with Christian theology without understanding the basically religious impulse that motivates it. For in this interpretation of rhetorical, cultic, and philosophical notions is to be found the profound conviction that what is original and ultimate in all being has found its way into man's soul. Here it leads to the perfection of this man in his moral, physical, and intellectual activities. As a function of the latter it leads to the insights for which all the great philosophers sought and which when found fulfill the self and give glory to God.

Here religion and culture come together. *Paideia* as the ideal that ancient Greece contributed to human history is carried on. The greatest works of art and literature as they participate in truth enhance human life. And human life in all its forms must rise to the heights known by the soul of the redeemed. Thus are the playwrights and poets learned in the schools drawn into Christian literature. They are seen as the precursors of true spirituality shared by all who have now been illumined. Rhetorical techniques so laboriously engrafted into the minds of school children are employed by Christian teachers to exhort and instruct the people in the moral tradition that is proper to free men. In short, the Christian theologian sees the church and its gospel crowning human civilization. Indeed, it is the schoolhouse of the human race.

Such humanism is not to be considered lightly. The phenomenon of Christian theology, whereby speaking of God is brought into such intimate connection with the fundamental or-

der of the world and man's place in it and whereby the traditions of the Judeo-Christian religion are seen as the key to
civilization, is a monument to the best in man's religious quest.
It is in addition, if we speak with Herrmann, an instance of
faith in which men sought to express in the language of their
own day what it means to have the sense of self-possession and
the call of moral responsibility in the future.

However, it also allied faith with knowledge in a way much
more akin to the provenance of the gospel of John than with
that of Paul, and here Herrmann would, I think, see the beginning of orthodoxy. For when one begins to work out a
scheme for understanding the work of Christ in the philosophic
form available in the Hellenistic world he runs the great risk
of becoming committed to certain particular notions which may
not take the test of time and may in a future age be either
wrong or irrelevant. Thus did the reflection about the Logos,
God, and the world begin to fall into patterns which were
taught by one generation to the next and became now themselves part of the tradition of the past. They were woven into
the interpretation of older tradition and thus also served as
vehicles for handing the past to those in the present.

Faith gradually becomes an affirmative response to the presentation of this tradition, although it is never completely isolated from the sense of freedom that connects it to Paul and
Jesus. The teaching office of the church comes finally to have
a theological undergirding that is the unique product of the development of Christianity in the Hellenized world. What had
been inherited from Judaism, namely, the scholarly study of
traditional material to bring it into connection with the on-
going life of the people of God, now becomes Christian philosophy in which man's intellectual quest reaches its goal in
a traditional set of ideas. Faith thus as trust in that which is
reliable becomes trust in the basic accuracy of a religiophilo-
sophical scheme. Faith it may yet be, but only a small step is
necessary to turn these traditional thoughts into orthodoxy.

CREEDALISM AND POLITICAL ESTABLISHMENT

Orthodoxy comes about when the traditions of the church that grew up to carry the inner life of Jesus along in the life of the community and provide the occasion for faith become both its content and criteria. This happens when certain ideas become fixed and certain expressions become indispensable for the maintenance of community existence.

It should be emphasized that this happens not only in theology but in the entire life of the church. Faith locked in the grip of moral, liturgical, or institutional practices is just as threatened as if it were fixed to the affirmation of set assertions. For these function correctly only when they bring one into the sort of self-possession in which he is disposed to be responsible for the future which dawns. Although liturgy, for example, may never have come significantly into Herrmann's writings, it can be argued on the basis of his thought that it is exactly here where the eschatological mysteries are rehearsed that the demand Jesus made upon his hearers for obedience is most adequately retained. And thus in this context can come faith as the living inner life of Jesus in the midst of his community. When, however, the liturgy becomes the enactment of the traditional for its traditional value, then faith is likely a casualty. The same may be said for moral traditions that may be the occasion for faith or that may be the greatest threat to faith.

But for orthodoxy to come about, there must be the opportunity in the life of the church to make traditions binding and have the sort of sanctions available for enforcing such action. The first prerequisite for such an opportunity is serious disagreement over the content of the church's teaching and the threat of splintering into rival groups that might each claim the tradition for its own. The second prerequisite is a concrete challenge to the man of faith in his world. The third prerequisite is the development of a movement large enough to involve the institutional problems of management, decisions about group life on a large scale, and the sense of identity with a rather comprehensive entity called " the church." Finally, the political structures must exist and be available to the Christian community for making and enforcing decisions on an " ecumenical " basis.

All these prerequisites were fulfilled in the Greco-Roman world by the time of Constantine and the legalization and establishment of the Christian religion in the Empire. Heresy and schismatic movements had given rise to the notion of a correct and incorrect way to possess and pass on the tradition. The resulting questions of episcopal authority, canon, and adequate formulation of theological topics had already been raised by the beginning of the third century. The general problem of the distinction of the Christian from the pagan mode of behavior made acute in time of persecution had been felt in the life of the church and had even caused serious and lasting divisions. The phenomenal growth of the church in the third century and its growing wealth certainly made increasingly evident the problems of organizing such a community, and the corresponding growth of ecclesiastical institutions provided evidence that church officials were equal to the task. Along with this, one finds the existence of synods, episcopal correspondence, and the like, which show the progress of ecumenical interest. With this came the refining of the notion of church as a comprehensive entity. When the political mechanism was provided by the imperial adoption of the Christian movement all the preconditions for orthodoxy were met.

In fact, it is with Constantine that we find the beginning of ecumenical councils where, in connection with the officers of the Empire, canons of creed and action were established which were considered binding upon the church universal. When this happens things have taken place which are of critical significance for the theological task, but which are often taken for granted in its exercise. There has been a wedding of theology and law in a way that determines how theology is done, what its topics will be, and its relation to its institutional context. The theological task has received what for centuries will be its definitive shape.

The transformation this makes in the theology of illumination which characterizes the meeting of Hebraic religion and Hellenic culture is remarkable. The balance which is in reality very delicate between the exercise of reasoning powers in search of the Logos and traditional declarations coming from the Jewish Bible and early Christian literature found in the enlightenment of the believer is now upset. And the formulations of this theology of illumination characteristic of Christian Platonism as they take their place in the tradition function now as prescriptions for faith rather than as the intellectual expression of freedom from the world found in redemption. Christian *paideia* is given its new destiny as catechetics.

To be sure, it takes centuries for the full implications of the establishment of an orthodoxy to be worked out in the educational scene. Not until the flourishing of catechetical manuals and methods in post-Tridentine Roman Catholicism and early Protestantism does Christian *paideia* reach its destiny. Furthermore, the drive toward true wisdom in faith never is entirely lost. Brilliant examples of Christian *paideia* such as the Cappadocians or Thomas Aquinas yet are to be found. But the theological side of this drive is so radically shaped by orthodox statements of faith that the close connection between the religious sense of deliverance into the realm of light and intellectual illumination is broken.

The nature of theological language is also significantly changed. Introduced into the theologian's perspective are creedal phrases carefully chosen from liturgical settings and edited to help solve a whole host of problems that have only oblique relation, if any, to the original liturgical exercise. For example, the *homoousios* in the Nicaean declaration is inserted into a creedal declaration not because it enhances the understanding or commitment of the one who might recite this on Baptism, but because it will help the church in council come to terms with controversy over the relationship between Son and Father. This controversy in turn involves not only disagreement over the nature of Christian religious experience, but argument about philosophical principles, and a large amount of personal pique.

In taking up the theological enterprise after Nicaea, one just is not free to engage in the kind of thought that led to the first book of Christian theology, Origen's *De Principiis*. Furthermore, he is not free from oversight by the bishop, since what he says may have real effect upon the struggles of the institutional church. And surely the secular arm under the efficient administration of the Constantinian Empire has more than just passing interest in his published expressions.

When thinking and writing in this sort of context, one is forced to come to terms with orthodox statements much in the way a lawyer and a judge must come to terms with constitutional pronouncements and legislative statute when facing a particular case of human conflict. In an analogous way the theologian must take the formulations of the church councils into his own thought and relate them to the structure of his ideas and the particular form of understanding which he finds meaningful and fruitful. That he really means by *homoousios* what Hosius did when he whispered it in Constantine's ear is really out of the question and a proposition that he would rather not consider lest the threat of heresy beset him.

The place of creedal materials in liturgy also changes, although this is much more difficult to isolate and discuss. For what the words of creeds recited by scores of Christians or listened to in the celebration of the priest by others actually mean to them can only be ascertained as this meaning is put into speech — an exercise that overlaps with but is by no means the same as theology. In a world where theology has become orthodoxy, this expression in speech may be shaped to fit the type of question that is asked. Over and above this is the difficulty of finding out how one ascertains meaning in religious and liturgical discourse. Nevertheless, the significance of creedal assertions in liturgical life for the man who also can do theology must include an intellectual element, and it is this element which is now affected by orthodox demands. The full implications of this, of course, are only seen in modern times with the breakdown of creedal orthodoxy.

By drawing the analogy between theology and legal arguments, I mean not to overstretch it. For peculiar to legal exegesis is the place courts of law have in the structure of society. Hence, legal doctrines abstract just enough from the specific case under adjudication to connect with customary patterns of action and other principles of social order. In theology tending toward orthodoxy, however, there still is at work the motivation toward knowledge that plays so great a part in the theology of illumination. Thus one grasps for knowledge so that his world may have order. And this order is closely related to the freedom of his soul. And exegesis of the tradition must be geared to the spiritual quest. So long as it does not frustrate this quest, the legal character of theology is not immediately clear, but it is still present.

One sees hints of this even as early as Origen, who remarks that the Trinitarian distinctions are fixed by tradition. With the filling out of these distinctions by the orthodox definitions and with the building up of canons of doctrine and action from the fourth century on, the room left for the speculative quest is relatively less, and the possibility of conflict between faith and the life of the mind is greatly increased. When this conflict comes, the really legal character of theological assertions comes shockingly to the fore.

Because its place in the church and perhaps the church's place in the social order are not as clearly and precisely fixed by customary action as the law and the courts, theology involves a looser exegesis of tradition than does the law. There is a wide latitude of expression from the rhetoric of the preacher, to the dialogue of the teacher, to the instruction of the catechist, to the political jockeying of the ecclesiastical officer, to the literary techniques of the man of letters. Within this latitude there are places for the continuation of the ideals of Greek *paideia,* philosophy, and science. Hardening into real legalism comes only when a fundamental challenge has been issued to the institution or institutions that have a proprietary interest in orthodoxy. Such a challenge, we shall see, does arise, but before we can consider it we must look a bit at the organization of tradition as itself a problem for the theologian.

THEOLOGY AS LEGAL EXEGESIS

What actually constitutes the tradition of the church has never been entirely clear. The adoption of Scriptures from the Jewish community by the early church was natural, since it was a segment of this community. However, there has been a discrepancy for many centuries between the Scriptures used in the synagogue and those read in the church. This canonical problem is accentuated with the growth of distinctly Christian Scriptures, and there has never been total accord about the limits and relative value of this corpus. In the main the decision about what will fall into an authoritative body of tradition deriving from pre-Christian and apostolic times has been a traditional decision. Relying upon a consensus of wide range and conciliar pronouncements largely in accord with this consensus, the church has formed a Bible.

What might be attached to the Bible as definitive of life and thought in the church is not to this day entirely clear. The collecting of materials from the fathers and from the important church synods was not an organized enterprise until well after the early period of church life. In fact, even the records of the first two great ecumenical councils, if they ever existed, have not been preserved. Thus the formation of a body of authoritative tradition alongside the Bible and in connection with which the Bible was read is not easy to detail or satisfactorily explained.

Nevertheless, one must speak of this body of tradition as something gradually taking shape in association with famous figures in the church, particularly gifted teachers, men such as Augustine, who had an eye to the preservation of their writings, and the actions of important bishops. These, along with and in explanation of the creedal declarations of the councils, begin to exercise authority over those who come after. Although the concreteness of declarations about action and ecclesiastical procedure makes the body of canon law more visible in embryo, a body of theological law is also taking shape.

Through the years the theological task is shaped by the presence of this tradition and becomes in an increasingly significant way legal exegesis. The particulars of this fact can only be clearly seen when one focuses upon the educational structures which were used by the church and the consequent influence they had upon the shape of the theological task.

When the separation from Judaism was relatively complete and the church was to be seen primarily as an institution in the Greco-Roman world, there was really no peculiarly Christian school system established. If there was a catechetical institute in Alexandria and if there were counterparts to this in other parts of the Empire, these were in no way rivals to the ordinary schools, nor were they engaged in general education. They were, rather, centers of study and research over and beyond ordinary classical training — now increasingly shaped by the rhetoricians — and they were designed to pursue the explanation of Judeo-Christian literature and perhaps to engage in Christian philosophy.[13] Except for polemical attack upon the idolatry of Hellenistic religion and some reservations about the morality reflected in classical literature, there was clear acceptance of the ideals and methods of Greek *paideia*. The various giants of patristic literature got their academic training, by and large, in the classical schools of antiquity.

Only with the decline of the school system in the Roman Empire and with the rise of church institutions either to serve particular functions or to replace the older schools, do we find the kind of educational setting in which theology, as one is more accustomed to think of it, is possible. Thus in the monastic communities or at the dawn of the medieval world in connection with the great cathedrals we find schools developed under the aegis of the church for instructing clergy, men in religious orders, or those who might be clerks in a society that was essentially ecclesiastically directed. Available for educational materials at this time was a body of literature which if not entirely oriented toward the concerns of the church at least was preserved for and colored by the church's intellectual and practical needs. What learning actually took place was in general geared to the transmission of past authorities with some eye to commenting upon them.

The brilliant revival of learning in the twelfth and thirteenth centuries is set, therefore, in a quite different institutional context from that of the early church fathers. Their theology of illumination is now reflected in the claim that all culture finds its perfection in the revealed truth borne by the church. This is supported by the fact that the church is the patron of culture. It is, therefore, hardly strange that with the revival of dialectic in the twelfth century the questions of logical categories, the metaphysical structure of the world, and the place of ideas in the mind of God would become intertwined and produce the debate over universals.[14] Theological ideas were so close at hand and so closely connected to the institution sponsoring learning that they could not be kept out. With them they brought the whole specter of heresy and served to keep the intellectual atmosphere charged, perhaps beyond warrant.

It was reflection upon dialectic and logic, however, which gave distinctive shape to the way theology would be done. Questions were raised and the various authorities who were held in repute were collated on the two sides of the question in order that a resolution of a seeming contradiction in the tradition might be resolved. This method of procedure, which may well have originated in dealing with Roman law,[15] came to brilliant fruition in Abelard and Peter Lombard. The former first used " theology " in a technical sense.[16] The latter's *Sentences* became the second enterprise of the scholar after he had learned to comment upon Biblical text. The dialectical method reached its apex, of course, in the *Summa Theologica* of Thomas Aquinas.

What is found here and what must surely strike the perceptive reader of Thomas is something quite akin to a legal brief. And the unification of *auctoritas* and *ratio* which is so close to the heart of the medieval Scholastic is really the accommodation of the tradition to the circumstances of contemporary learning in order to make it manageable and useful. Thus the analogy to the law is no deprecation of theology as practiced by the great medievals but rather a recognition of a genius to make use of learning in a particular context to make vital the traditions that support key institutions. Nothing less than this is characteristic of just law.

It was not thought until later in the medieval period that *auctoritas* and *ratio* might eventually come into conflict. The confidence that this was so reflected the power exercised by the theology of illumination and its various themes. These were transmitted to the medievals, of course, by Augustine's espousal of them, and his particular brand of Christian Platonism helps nurture the life and thought of Latin Christendom. Thus the connection with the perfection of human reasoning of redemption and the freedom which comes with illumination is still to be found — especially in Anselm. Whether one can account for the weakening of Augustinianism or indeed indicate the extent to which it is weakened by pointing to a rather more empirically oriented epistemology in medieval Aristotelianism is beyond our interest here. Nevertheless, the separation of nature as an area open to the free exercise of human reason from supernatural things made known only in traditional sources of revelation and then clarified by reason must raise the possibility that *auctoritas* and *ratio* may not always be in accord. In this case, faith is transformed from *fides quaerens intellectum* into the virtue of one who responds knowingly to grace.

When the conflict between *auctoritas* and *ratio* cannot be resolved and comes into the open, then the real implications of the original Johannine provenance are made evident. Faith as response to the declaration of the church, even though it involves the realignment of one's existence in the world, involves him in the problem of knowing and incorporates into the understanding of faith commitment to the particular world in which faith arose.

Theology comes into being as a consequence of the church's following out this Johannine provenance. In the Western church it comes to brilliant glory in the medieval period. But here in connection with the comprehensive institution of the church it operates within specific limitations and is made to serve specific ends. When with the appearance of the independence which is characteristic of human inquiry these limits are crowded, fundamental questions about the theological enterprise are raised. Actually, these questions are so fundamental that they are not yet today clearly seen and certainly have not been clearly answered.

Nevertheless, where the techniques by which the tradition was made to be reasonable to medieval men were successful and where this legal exegesis was both sophisticated and ingenious, Christian theology is a monument to faith. It indicates how the religious power deriving from Jesus might lead men to form institutions to further the common life and educational methods to nurture the understanding. That this whole world might pass is no threat to faith, but such passing certainly raises questions about whether theology will remain fixed to the traditional forms of church and school or whether there is not some place apart from orthodoxy where faith might come to expression.

In standing so determinedly against orthodoxy Herrmann was insisting that the theological task was reshaped by important events which called in question the medieval synthesis. We can, I think, follow behind him, pausing to pay tribute to the monumental character of this synthesis and yet insisting that it finally had to come apart in modern history. In fact, we can argue with Herrmann that the life of faith itself necessitated leaving orthodoxy behind. But with these assertions we have arrived at Luther.

CHAPTER FOUR

Luther and Reformation in Theology

NO MATTER ON WHICH SIDE of the great divide in Western Christendom one stands, he may still refer to the movements of the sixteenth century as Reformation, for fundamental transformations in the church took place then which changed rather radically the structure of church life. On the one hand, the medieval church became the Roman Catholic Church as the temporal claims of the papacy were widely curtailed and institutional forms grew up for becoming an international body. On the other hand, national churches came into existence, many of which claimed to have broken fundamentally with Rome over the issue of what really constitutes the Christian gospel.

No little confusion still exists about the nature of the Reformation and no single characterization of it will in any way do to illumine the diverse movements that were afoot. Once again, therefore, if one wishes to turn to this particular period of history and claim that things are reshaped by the events which took place, he must clearly delineate his point of reference. For Herrmann, this was Luther. And in this he shared a certain predilection with others in recent theology for seeing in the life and thought of this particular great Reformer a rediscovery of the gospel and a tapping again of the wellsprings of Christian religious life.

As Herrmann puts it: Luther came to a comprehension of Christianity " amid the inward battles of a soul that could find no rest in any means of grace, because it sought the God of grace Himself, and amid such struggle he discovered records in the sacred Scriptures of what it is that can redeem a man." [1] Or, in other words, he came to faith in the struggle to find a gracious God, having recourse to the Bible where he found impulses to faith in the work of the redeeming Christ.

For Herrmann, this is to discover again the primary religiousness of the Christian as he comes to personal self-awareness and possession, finding in the process that God and neighbor are personalized too. Luther in his struggle to find himself a justified man found a gracious God who in the person of Jesus offered him the love and forgiveness he felt everywhere else denied. The resulting trust and confidence he called faith, and speaking of justification in this faith, he was also able to speak of a new moral disposition being created so that one could go forth as a Christ to his neighbor.

This experience came to Luther as he studied the Scriptures, and Herrmann is quick to point out that the natural authority which the Scriptures had for him as well as the whole world of thought common to the medieval church provide the backdrop for any portrayal of his spiritual quest. To this backdrop one might add the whole world of medieval piety from which Luther drew so much and which even in reaction he in large measure retained.

Nevertheless, Herrmann wishes to distinguish between Luther's experience of faith and his attempt to raise the Bible into a position of authority over against the other forms of tradition found in the fathers and institutionally centered in the papacy. In my terms this would entail a distinction between a Pauline notion of faith and the subtle transformation of this in Johannine writings. For in faith one participates in full human life under the influence of Jesus and the community that passes on his inner life. In making faith response to revelation — even though this be of Christ as Redeemer — one shifts faith from personal trust and confidence to trust in a tradition. In Luther the tradition of the Bible provides the vehicle for a personal word to be addressed to him by God. Thus he keeps the Johannine view of faith together with the Pauline. It is the latter, however, that Herrmann wishes to designate as essential to the reformation he sees centered in Luther. In it is the rediscovery of the gospel.

This should not be misunderstood as subjectivism. Herrmann is quick to anticipate a certain stylized criticism of Luther and notes that Luther's experience of faith can only be understood when one sees that he is overwhelmed by the objective power which comes to him from the man Jesus.[2] Subjectivism is a charge that can be leveled at Luther only when one tries to understand faith as response to revelation. Then a subject-object structure is introduced which forces one to speak of *fides quae creditur* and *fides qua creditur*. Only when faith and subjectivity are related as Herrmann sees them will one recognize that both are created by the action of a gracious God, and this comes from outside oneself.

To assert the distinction, however, between Luther's experience of faith and his justifying this on the basis of the authority of Scripture is to provide an interesting means for understanding his reforming activities. For Luther was not just rebellious. He reacted to those things which threatened faith whether they might be pope, emperor, scholasticism, Erasmus, or enthusiasts. And all his reactions had the character of *ad hoc* decisions reflecting a consistency only when one sees that the gospel of forgiveness was at stake. But this consistency is striking and gives heart to one who reflects on the seemingly contradictory assertions of Luther clothed, as these often are, in violent or coarse language.

It is not just an attempt to interpret Luther's reforming activities that motivates Herrmann to distinguish between his faith and the Scriptural principle he erects. Herrmann wishes to argue that the theological consequences of faith were never really worked out by Luther. Part of the confusion of the Reformation in its Protestant form results from this fact. Many of the things that transpired did nothing to enhance faith and even did much to inhibit it. With this the genuine impulses for reform were lost and faith was engulfed in new institutions and subjected to a new orthodoxy.

When, however, one returns to faith in order to speak of what was really at stake in Luther's discovery of the gospel, he finds an interesting perspective for assessing what happens to the theological task in the period of the Reformation and how it is rather radically reshaped.

LEARNING AND HUMAN SELF-AWARENESS

From the days of the early Sophists men have wrestled with the realization that education means not just the passing along of customs and traditions but the preparation of the student to exercise independent judgments. This, however, necessitates learning the means by which men normally make judgments and justify their independence to others. Thus within the educational enterprise is contained a struggle between rote learning or what may be popularly — if indeed incorrectly — called scholasticism and the drive of the individual self to comprehend its world and dispose of its destiny.

Simple generalizations have been made about periods in human history in the light of this struggle. The medieval age has been contrasted to the Renaissance as scholasticism is contrasted to the drive for individuality. Obviously, such a generalization is too facile and the issue is far more complex. The High Middle Ages actually contained tremendous diversity, and one finds in pursuing the study of men like Thomas Aquinas remarkable individuality and ingeniousness in using traditional methods and conceptions. By the same token not all the literary men of the Italian fifteenth century were original or creative and many were as " scholastic " in temperament as any hidebound Franciscan.[3]

Nevertheless, what men have tried to indicate by such a generalization has some limited validity. There was in the intellectual movements of the fourteenth and fifteenth centuries beginning in Italy and spreading to northern Europe in the following centuries a growing awareness of the importance of the individual and the unique, the novel and the historical. Developing from this was a deep suspicion of the traditional justified as such.

There would be another spurious generalization involved in the attempt to characterize Luther's Reformation as the struggle between law and gospel and to see law as embodied in the papal church to which he reacted in the name of the individual freedom that comes through the gospel. However, there is a rough correspondence between this generalization and the facts of the case. The organs of tradition can in many instances become servants of the devil holding man in bondage to sin and to the hopeless task of trying to win his salvation. The gospel and its word of forgiveness may then actually deliver one from these strictures into the full freedom of faith and the full power of his individual being. If this is true, as it seemed to be in Luther's case, then it can be argued that there is at work in both Renaissance and Reformation forces which will eventually call fundamentally in question the authority of the traditional.

Nevertheless, the events in question do not make this argument completely secure. For the particulars of the Renaissance are as complicated as those of the Reformation. Whereas it was in Italy largely a lay matter associated with life in the cities, it was in northern Europe and Spain closely connected with the church. Men such as Erasmus saw Jerome and Valla as their predecessors and subjected their learning to the task of restoring simple Christianity. Furthermore, skepticism might lurk alongside credulity, for amid the zest for learning was also fascination with the occult and the mysterious. In certain universities the literary faculty might be widely separated from the theological faculty. In others the literary skills, especially in Greek and Hebrew, were introduced into the instruction of theological candidates.

Like so many other things in human history, the Renaissance sprang perhaps as much as anything from a subtle change in educational priorities. Whereas in the centuries previous dialectic had emerged from the basic liberal arts as the tool for appropriating the learning from the past, now grammar and rhetoric overhauled it.[4] Methods of literary analysis developed that focused upon the way things were said and upon philological insight. Arising from this was a growing criticism of the scholar who makes use of writings from the past without becoming conscious of the author's particular style and the context that gives meaning to his words.

This is the root of modern historical consciousness where in examining the records of the past one begins to hear the author speaking his own language in his own day. In a way already perceived by the men of the Renaissance this brings with it a certain new self-awareness. For events and men in the past stand off at a distance and force one to see the peculiarities of his own situation. A different mind-set results; the traditional now becomes the historical, and no longer will the marvelous tool of dialectic forged by the ingenious men of the medieval period serve to bring the traditional into relevance for the present. Another form of expression built upon philological and literary analysis is necessary, perhaps making great use of rhetoric.

For Luther this was the living word. He was at one with the humanists in trying to hear the words of Scripture so that they might be a word speaking to him. From this he characterized the church as a " mouth house " where the Word of God is found.

Luther was highly sympathetic toward the methods of the humanistic scholars, learning Greek and Hebrew himself, translating the Bible, and rejoicing in the presence of such scholars as Melanchthon at Wittenberg. He also forged his own hermeneutical tools from those, like Faber Stapulensis, who had reduced the fourfold exegesis of medieval times to a twofold method whereby one sought for the historical sense of a text on the one hand and the sense in which it might be spiritually alive in the present on the other.[5] This latter was for Luther as it preached Christ. In this he displayed skill both as a literary critic and as an expositor.

Now, it must be emphasized that the fourfold exegesis was not unconcerned with historical evidence and the literal meaning of the text. It must not be underestimated as a tool for making the ancient Scriptures of use in a rather different context. But once again the subtle change of emphasis away from dialectical skills of argumentation and analysis and toward literary and philological criticism gives birth to a quite different attitude toward written texts.

Luther, it would seem, never really came to terms with the implications of this change. He did deny the authority of the tradition that had developed since Biblical times for interpreting the Bible unless it was authentic to the gospel. Furthermore, he capitalized on the notion which had been present for some time that of all the church traditions the Bible was most important. Indeed, he reflected upon the criteria for delineating a canon. But he seems not to have reflected on the character of the Bible itself as tradition. He assumed, as did even the humanists, that the primitive records might bring one closest to Christ. Although for Luther there was great concern that the Christ of whom the Scripture bore witness be contemporaneous with him, and although he had a special talent for weaving peculiarly Saxon elements into Biblical narratives without destroying their original force, he still shared with Erasmus the notion that the traditions of the primitive church were more authentic and authoritative for the Christian religion than those of later Christendom. He never really followed through the inclination which led him to be suspicious of James, Hebrews, Jude, and Revelation and ask whether indeed this did not call the very Scriptural principle itself in question.

Yet Luther had really very different interests from a humanist like Erasmus. For the Bible was important as living word because he heard himself addressed through it by the God who in his deity forgives and transforms his creature. This forgiveness is known anew in every moment as the Word lives. Thus the Bible is Bible only as it is gospel; and the gospel is gospel as it is preached; and preaching takes place only when one is called to faith. Speech for Luther is important as it is living speech, not as it is classical. To this perhaps can be attributed his love of German and his joy in speaking in the vernacular.

Can this not be called true humanism? [6] For Luther follows through in certain ways the implications of the reemphasis upon grammar whereby one becomes conscious of the living character of speech. The words and expressions of men arise out of the situations in which they live, giving form, shape, and manageability to experience. To feel the wonder and mystery of man, the speaking and hearing one, is to feel closely the mystery of life itself. The humanist who becomes an antiquarian is no humanist at all but a pedant; he is a scholastic in the pejorative sense of that word. Luther in his attitude toward the Bible and the conclusions about man in relationship to God which he drew from his experience of being addressed by the Word was a true humanist.

But Luther was also a traditionalist. And here the ambiguity of his relationship to the Renaissance is seen. For in certain areas of experience he was blind to the peculiarities of human novelty and history. Where the traditional way of seeing things was not drawn into conflict with faith, he saw no need to call it in question. And even where he did call it in question the means — such as the Scriptural principle — might be themselves traditionally sanctioned. Thus it is not easy to see many of the tendencies of Renaissance thinkers in accord with Luther's own thought. Yet it need not deter us from arguing that the historical consciousness begotten by the study of writings in their own context is in harmony with Luther's experience that God is only real and gracious to the man who has heard his call and come into faith. And the case may be made that it is really the man of faith who in the fullness of his own self-possession is best equipped to see the individuality of other human selves. As God has come to him in Christ, so may he go out to others as a Christ to his neighbor.

This is the case Herrmann wished to make. He did not thereby wish to be a strict Lutheran, however. For he argued that the Scriptural principle for challenging the authority of the Roman Catholic Church brought with it as many difficulties as it solved. Because of it, Luther's understanding of faith could not be fully effective in theology. One must pursue this argument in order to understand the odd shape given the theological task.

THE PATH TO RIGID ORTHODOXY

The fact that Luther and after him Melanchthon were both Reformers and university professors points out the two pressures that theology experienced. These had been present from the very beginning when the ideals of *paideia* were seen to be fulfilled by the illumination one received from the Logos incarnate. They were present in Augustine, the bishop and the man in quest of true understanding. They were reflected in the great Scholastics who ingeniously adapted Aristotle to the Augustinian synthesis. The one is for a clear and consistent way of viewing things that may be taught to others in the attempt to bring them into possession of their world. The other is to take an institution and the tradition which both gives this institution its self-identity and is borne along by it and make them continually relevant to one's contemporaries.

The role of the school in this process of managing a tradition and nurturing an institution has never been clear. This is partly because the role of education in drawing men into customary life or in giving birth to their individuality is itself confused. And one can see surrounding almost all of the great figures in theology a certain cloud of uneasiness generated by those ecclesiastical brethren who sense in their individual understanding of things a threat to the traditional. The line between orthodoxy and heresy is usually perilously thin.

In the case of Luther but even more so with Melanchthon the dual roles of educator and reformer are not separated and thus the theological task is set within the marriage of church and university. Changes in the university curriculum, the working out of textbooks and means of instruction, and the content of discussions are all in part determined by considerations of ecclesiastical reform. The introduction of more humanistic studies may actually come from other sources but it can be justified on grounds of interpreting Holy Scripture. The shift in exegetical styles may actually be borrowed from men who were at home in the Roman Catholic Church, but it is undergirded by a theology of the Word. Debates within and between faculties are aroused by the struggle for reform and not solely by intellectual issues.

Of course, no university has led a life of removal from the issues of its day, but the paroxysms that seized Europe in the sixteenth and seventeenth centuries were extreme enough — especially in Germany — to involve the universities even more so than in other days. In Protestant lands where new universities came into existence and where there was extensive work on the development of schools no small consideration was given to the role the university might play in defining the contours of Protestantism and passing on its substance to new generations.[7] In Catholic lands it was no less true what with the work of the Jesuits founding colleges and with the new conception of strictly Roman institutions of higher learning.

The political upheavals of this era are of great consequence for the educational enterprise as well. The international character of university life is shattered and the entanglement of the Reformation in rising national consciousness, the disintegration of medieval feudalism, and the creation of new civil authorities is reflected intensely in the life of the universities. For the Protestant, this is especially evident in the lands of the German Reformation.

That the forces which were originally at work in the creation of orthodoxy are now felt is immediately obvious. Creedalism is just more complex as men on the one hand try to identify with what is ancient and traditional and yet on the other hand try to distinguish themselves from other Christians who also claim the ancient and traditional for their own. That means to support one's case are worked out in study and research only makes orthodoxy more scholastic. This need not necessarily condemn it, but it reinforces the legal character of the theological enterprise. Argument proceeds along the lines taken by the judge and advocate.

For Protestantism this makes for a very difficult situation. Luther had called the Bible — one segment of tradition — over against the tradition of the church for which the pope claimed responsibility. The effect was to limit the use that could be made of great thinkers in the church — even the beloved Augustine — in defending one's declaration of belief. But it also created in a smaller way the very same problem that beset the Scholastics of the High Middle Ages. For there is ambiguity if indeed not contradiction in the Biblical text. Thus it is necessary to come to a consensus understanding of the fundamental content of the gospel and set this out in some definitive form. Faith in consequence is threatened by the possible fate of becoming subscription to creeds [8] even though these creeds claim Biblical sanction.

In addition to this the theological enterprise must come to terms with its own tradition. By this time the effect of the medieval universities cannot be ignored. For theology has developed a literature, a method of discussion and examination, and sets of problems and conceptions that have for several centuries been passed on from one generation of scholars to another. Furthermore, the theologians are a special faculty with their own prerogatives and their own standards of initiation and evaluation. Protestant theologians are not cut off from this tradition and in fact use it very considerably. But they weave into the traditional problems and traditional language a new set of issues coming out of the peculiar circumstances of the Reformation. The result is the production of minute distinctions, very fixed terms of expression, rigid division into schools of thought, and the like which give to the word " scholasticism " its distasteful quality. When one sees that these controversies and discussions are supported not only by the events in ecclesiastical history which make up the Reformation but also by loyalties to teacher and school which are part of university life, then he can see how really confused the theological task has become.

The picture is not exactly the same in Roman Catholic lands but it is not radically different. Three things at least do, however, provide for some distinction. First of all, the need to break with tradition over the question of Biblical authority is not felt strongly.[9] Secondly, the university is not brought so clearly under the leadership of the theological faculty. The earlier pattern coming from the Middle Ages whereby the arts faculty really controlled the university continues to prevail [10] except in the few cases where Catholic universities are founded. Thirdly, the existence of time-honored lines of authority in the church, a pattern of adjudicatory bodies alongside the nation-state for handling ecclesiastical business, and the separation of function between the university professor and the bishop, all helped to temper the scholastic mood. The absence of institutional clarity within the various Protestant groups, the searching for means of self-identity in them, and the uneasiness that a prophetic movement must always have about its relationship to traditional patterns of order all helped to make Protestantism — both Lutheran and Reformed — vulnerable to rigid orthodoxy and its academic handmaiden — scholasticism.

To this can be added, finally, the tendency which is latent in every theology of the Word to wed religious experience to matters of the intellect. The Protestant rebellion against the sacramental piety of the Roman Catholic Church may not be a necessary result of Luther's rediscovery of the gospel in the living word of the Bible. Nevertheless, when the two are together and there is special emphasis placed upon preaching in the life of the church, the intellectual life is elevated to greater prominence and understanding becomes the prerequisite — in some measure at least — of piety. In Calvinist much more than in Lutheran lands this happens and it has great effect in the shaping of the theological task.

Perhaps the contrast between the scholasticism of the High Middle Ages and that of rigid orthodoxy can be seen by pointing out the different place of philosophy in the two. In the medieval university philosophy had developed in the arts faculty largely around the problems of logic. It had taken on certain characteristics of its own and pursued its own problems. The more metaphysical interests that attracted the theologians especially with the reintroduction of Aristotle in the thirteenth century did not necessarily dovetail with the philosophical practices of the arts faculty. Since the great theologians were members of religious orders and forbidden to teach in the arts faculty in Paris, the use made of Aristotle was really within the province of theology as a tool for organizing the tradition and making it intelligible.

In the later Middle Ages and on into the sixteenth and seventeenth centuries many things contributed to the development of philosophy. The possession of all of Aristotle's writings, the founding of nonuniversity centers such as the Academy of Florence devoted to the study of Plato, the rudimentary scientific work in the area of cosmology and physics, and the growing tendencies toward specialization, all led to an independence of philosophy itself. Finally, it separated from the arts into a faculty of its own with the appropriate degrees and procedures.[11]

However, in the circles of the Reformation and Counter-Reformation, the arts faculty of the university is made to serve as a training ground for those who proceed to the higher faculties — especially and chiefly theology. Thus the philosophical enterprise is made to serve as the handmaiden to the queen of the sciences in such a way that the theories of Aquinas about reason and faith receive their first real institutional implementation. Specifically in the setting of the German Reformation through the work of Melanchthon, Aristotle is given establishment status, helping to make Lutheran orthodoxy unbending toward the new physics and cosmology which had developed out of the independent philosophical tradition.[12]

This use of philosophy by theologians to serve their cause has not only given rise to misshaped problems such as faith and reason, philosophy and theology, Bible and science, it has also belied a real misunderstanding of the philosophical task by theologians in general. Not the least reason for this is the fact that theology was originally the creation of the philosophers — a creation which in its Christian setting grew to dominate and control its maker. The first Christian theologians were happy to call themselves philosophers and saw the perfection of the quest for the understanding of deity in the incarnate Logos. What they did, however, was to fix certain philosophical terms and notions and certain physical and metaphysical schemes within the tradition of the church. With the coming of orthodoxy these in turn were subject to the sort of legal exegesis which became theology.

When philosophy regained a certain independence partly through the specification of learning and the divisions in the university and partly through the new culture of the Renaissance, its place in the theological tradition was bound to become unclear. That this state of affairs continues is only evidence that the theological task although changed in the Reformation was not reflected upon sufficiently to see its real shape.

To say all this, of course, is not necessarily to lose sight of the fact that not all theology — in the broader sense of the word — is settled in the university and therefore scientific. Here the role of Luther, Melanchthon, and Salvin as *reformers* should be reemphasized. For the attempt to articulate the implications of one's faith in the life of the community of Christians and thus to perpetuate faith is basic to the renewal of the Christian religion in the time of the Reformation. But reflection upon the kind of institution which might implement this part of the theological enterprise which was never clearly undertaken, and thus what might have been reformation in theology, became instead the opening for moribund orthodoxy. Here, I think, is where Herrmann's case rests.

HUMANISM AND RELIGION

The experience of faith in which one discovers himself justified by a forgiving God and thus empowered in his trust and confidence in the goodness of God to act for himself in the affairs of men is the source of true humanism. This assertion rests on Herrmann's analysis of faith and indicates what stands at the center of the Christian religion. Implied in it is the claim that what follows on the Renaissance and Reformation, forming and conditioning the modern world view, is really at one with the religious impulses of Christianity mediated by Luther.

To make the argument in this fashion is to admit along with Herrmann that theology did not follow along. For the churches were concerned to assert their self-identity by the means of confessional precision and were set on condemning their enemies by showing them heretics. The resonance for this sort of squabbling in the universities was such as to give it the external trappings of serious intellectual labor. Nevertheless, the legal aspect of theological argument is now fully in command and the vicissitudes of political conflict must be seen far to outweigh the concerns for real understanding of man in his world. In fact where there was fruitfulness at all in theological work it is found in connection with political and social theory.

At this point we venture out onto a no-man's-land heavily mined and exceedingly treacherous. Not the least adding to the danger of this ground is the rugged terrain of modern intellectual history. Pitfalls are to be found wherever one speaks too glibly of causality and the pretentious trap of religious apologetic beckons. It is easy to claim too much and insist that Luther and the Reformation stand at the fountainhead of modern culture and that the freedom of faith makes possible the freedom of inquiry and action so celebrated now as secularization.[18]

To avoid disaster in this no-man's-land I wish to make a much more limited argument adhering, I believe, to the path blazed by Herrmann. I want to insist along with him that

Protestant orthodoxy was a serious misreading of Luther's religious insight, even though he through insistence upon the Scriptural principle was in large measure responsible for opening this way. Beyond this I want to insist that his experience of faith actually affords one the most adequate way for coming to terms with the intellectual explosion of the Enlightenment. This is a happy circumstance for the man who finds no home in classical orthodoxy. But it is also indicative of the problem of truly assessing the theological task. For now the one who follows out the implications of his faith, seeking to communicate it to others, finds himself in a tenuous position. He stands with one foot inside the theological tradition where the heritage of the church is passed along and with the other foot on the shifting ground of modern intellectual life.

One aspect of this is illustrated by the fact that men today returning to the medieval or Reformation period have a reasonable idea where theological problems are to be found and what might constitute their answers. When one looks to the modern period beginning at least by 1650, he is less sure what is a theological problem, who defines it, what sort of literature presents it, what might constitute an answer, and whose answer commands any authority. This is true on Protestant soil but is no less so in Roman Catholic countries — witness a Pascal. And in both the relative positions of laity and clergy are unclear enough to cause additional perplexity.

To be sure, the external facts of secularization are partly responsible for this confusion brought upon the inquirer. The new dynamics of church and state vying for authority and seeking stable relationships, the rise of science and technology and the expansion of horizons with the contact with different cultures, and all the other aspects of modernity add variables to intellectual equations which make them all but insoluble. The culmination of the movement begun in the Italian Renaissance, where learning was taken outside the formal school and into the circle of the wealthy urban merchant, furthered by the invention of printing and the dissemination of information to more and more people, came with the spread of intellectual activity to many who had loose or at best ambiguous relationships with the university or college. Different standards of evaluation about the quality of this intellectual activity were born. The acceptability to court, middle-class circle, salon, or sect might in large measure determine adequacy and truth.

Material that was previously the province of academic theology, for example, might be taken over into new cultural settings where it was looked at in a somewhat different way, served a quite different function, and was evaluated with rather different standards. Protestantism especially, with its close identification with certain new centers of political power, with — at least in Calvinism — its association with the urban middle class, and with its great emphasis upon the place of preaching in church life necessitating a learned or semilearned clergy, provides a quite unusual setting for doing theology. The theological task is thus newly reshaped.

Reflecting this more external condition is a movement in the history of ideas in which men outside the canons of the university ask about judgment, method, order, and truth. This gives rise to aspects of modern science but is not restricted to it. All kinds of new thought and speculation arise in reflection upon and exchange of ideas about man and his world. These, of course, penetrated the schools and could not be unrelated to the institutions which fostered skills in reading, writing, and thinking. Nevertheless, there is evident a new freedom from the traditions that tend finally to govern any important and successful institution.

Theologically important was the reflection on nature that eventually saw its perfection lying not beyond it but within it.[14] Thus the whole idea of cosmic order depending upon the completion of nature by grace was challenged. As an alternative, one proposed that nature is complete in itself and the job of human knowledge is to find its order and express this as clearly and precisely as possible. The confidence that one could do this was founded upon his success in predicting and managing nature as a result of it. Whether he might be adhering to traditional notions is of only secondary concern at best. Whether he might also be calling in question the idea of nature as an entity with an overall order is another matter which finally arose.

The import of this new idea of nature is not just that it challenged a traditional way of viewing man and the world he lived in accepted by both Catholic and Protestant scholastics. This, of course, was serious enough and has been the source of several centuries of acrimonious bickering between the representatives of theism and naturalism. But its real significance lies in its fundamental disinterest in the sanction of tradition. Truth, if we may sound very contemporary, is a function of usefulness. Or, if we may sound very old, man is the measure of all things.

Perhaps the allusion to Sophist doctrine here is not at all out of order. For these great founders of education can be seen as rebels against tradition who asked the questions of truth and goodness in such a way as to call custom to the bar.[15] Much of the modern spirit is a rebirth of " sophistication " with the irony that history has made education customary. The critical spirit thus is introduced back into the educational tradition, demanding a justification of understanding and learning in the immediacy of the present.

Of course, one is not always clear about the man who now claims to be the measure of all things. And here the question about true humanism becomes extremely vital. What is it indeed that leads to the understanding of man and how can one come to the decisions of value about his state in the world? How does one get clear the possibilities and frailties of humankind? Surely it is not unfair to say that it is much easier to detach nature from grace than to assess exactly what has been accomplished here and what place man might have in a world which is now radically reconstructed. Freedom becomes a rather heavy burden to bear.

Once again Luther and his experience of faith becomes extremely relevant. The venture into this world in trust and confidence, knowing that only as one has to come to terms with his own individuality as a creature and become oriented around a conscience, is indeed a frightful thing in which one is constantly under attack. But it is also a glorious existence resting upon the gracious, creative power of God. From this stance, man is a many-sided being whose essence is available only to the one who has sensed the uniqueness of individual men and the novelty of their historical life. His management of his world, although his distinct responsibility, is always conditioned by the particular problems and interests which assume importance at particular times and places.

It is this humanism which ties together the historical consciousness born in the Renaissance and the drive for independence in thought and judgment so important for the Enlightenment. Luther is a significant focal point, although by no means the only one, for viewing their connection. Furthermore, the religious impulses of the Christian religion funneled through him can be seen to have implemented their success, albeit in ambiguous relationship to the institutions of the church that he helped to found.

In common spirit with these attempts to find the truly human while being sensitive to the historical character of human existence is the attempt to assess the nature of man's religiousness. Thus is revived a question that was of special importance to some of the early church fathers who wrote in Latin: How does the Christian gospel stand *vis-à-vis religio?* The latter by the Christian era had come to mean not only the external actions of devotion to the gods but also the internal character of devotion itself.[16] In the church's message about Jesus the Christ, the acts of worship and discipline fostered by his community, and the particular patterns of devotion and reverence connected to it the church fathers of the patristic era saw proper or true *religio* and defended it as such.

In the Renaissance and Reformation the question of true *religio* is raised again after being for nearly a millennium outside of men's purview. On the one hand, this comes from Platonic interest in ideal religion (or piety) in the Italian Renaissance;

on the other, it comes from the struggle of the Reformers to define for themselves and others what constitutes proper religiousness when the traditional institution, its practices, attitudes, and doctrines are under fire. Although, perhaps for linguistic reasons, the discussion took place mostly on Calvinist soil, it seems to me to be a question that must be raised by any Protestant who has thought through Luther's conception of faith.

Interestingly enough, Calvin's great work *Christianae religionis institutio*, rendered by Smith *Grounding in Christian Piety*,[17] is a summary of church doctrine edited according to Reformed principles. It would seem reasonable to draw the inference that proper religiousness depends upon being adequately instructed in sound doctrine. Thus it should be no surprise to find that by the time one reaches the Enlightenment, religion has come to be identified with doctrine and like all human traditions has been subjected to scrutiny. Naturally, this scrutiny must lead one to ask about the special character of this tradition, its general adequacy before the canons of human reasoning, and finally about its being historically conditioned.

All the quarrels that are spawned about religion in general, natural and revealed religion, Christian and non-Christian religions, and the like — quarrels that continue until today — are based upon the kind of development in the concept religion which was really underdevelopment. Perhaps the presence of Protestant scholasticism was not a negligible factor in causing this, but in fact the confessionalism that infested the Reformation made it impossible for Protestants to reflect carefully on the real question involved. Thus they did not ask about the character of proper piety and were grossly insensitive to the tremendous implications for religion in their criticism of sacramental orders and their massive commitment to preaching and the word.

These various factors in modern intellectual history crisscross one another to create the bewildering mass of problems we confront. They also have so affected the theological task that it has almost no shape at all. But unfortunately they do not account for all of the difficulty. For we must not overlook the fact that in Protestantism especially, but also in the mission work of the Roman Catholic Church as well, the exercise of preaching and the communication of the gospel have had remarkable effect. This too does things to theology.

THEOLOGY BETWEEN RHETORIC AND SCIENCE

The relationship between faith and speech is subtle and must be dealt with very carefully. This is in large measure due to the fact that expression in words is so important for the realization of human life that it comes close to being essential for it. Indeed, without speaking and hearing it is difficult to imagine men. Since faith in its Pauline sense as rediscovered by Luther is also bound up closely with the realization of human life, it is natural to see it intimately related to speech. We have already noticed how the dynamic quality of speaking and hearing was for Luther paradigmatic of the basic relationship between God and man. What we must resist, however, is the temptation to build a mythology about language. Is it not the case that the living quality of speech derives from the living quality of selves? To be sure, it is the means for selves to receive definition and clarity, and this is important for selfhood. But the center of the self remains yet at the origination of speech, and speech serves or fails to serve the self's purposes.

Although these few words are not at all meant to solve the complicated problem of speech and selfhood, they will suffice to indicate that from a Herrmannian point of view faith takes priority over the communication of faith in speech. It is faith which lives in the Christian community in the inner life of Jesus, and the communication of this faith is complete only if men are renewed and made centers of responsible action from it.

Thus we must get clearly before us the fact that speech is sometimes meaningful in what it does and sometimes meaningful in what it says. Roughly speaking, the former may be associated with rhetoric and the latter with science.[18] For from ancient times men have fostered the art of speaking with primary interest in what this might accomplish for them and how it might help in ordering the common life. From ancient times men have also resisted the rhetorician and have asked whether his word was indeed true. Human culture has seen this struggle carried on; the educational system has lived with it constantly. And no resolution of this problem is in sight, for it touches too closely the quality of the life one lives.

Expressions of faith may lay claim to being science or they may be rhetoric. Part of the task of the theologian in the modern world is to evaluate these claims. His task is made difficult by the Johannine-rooted theology of the Word. For now that which gives contour and order to the world, seen to be declared in Jesus of Nazareth, is connected intimately to the preaching of the church. This not only puts one on the road to orthodoxy which we have described, it also commits him to making scientific claims for his speech and avoiding recognition of its rhetorical quality.

Perhaps this is a blessing — the blessing of innocence — for consciousness of rhetoric and its power in the common life does not lead to comfort. It may lead to cynical use of rhetorical art in the attempt to work one's will. It may lead to moral scruples when one faces the raw power that the clever use of speech puts in his hands. But it can never lead to naïve unawareness of the explosive force that skill in speaking contains.

Rhetorical arts have served the church well in its innocence. The power to convince men of the adequacy of the message about Jesus the Christ and all the interpretative apparatus of Christian expression and to bring them into a community which through keeping his inner life alive has given tremendous impetus to Western culture is not to be lightly evaluated. Nor is it to be impugned. For the moral fabric of this community has done many great things to humanize man and to bring him to consciousness of his responsibility in the world and his power to make history. In modern times, in Protestant lands especially, the remarkable things done through rhetoric — both spoken and written — in the interests of further extension of this religious and moral influence should not be dismissed cavalierly. In America from the Puritans through the great waves of revival which swept the continent to Martin Luther King the fruitful use of rhetorical skills is of no little significance. To this day they are exercised in certain quarters of our church life with not entirely deleterious effect.

Nevertheless, we must come to terms with the loss of innocence. For to recognize rhetoric as the use of speech not just for its meaning but for what it can accomplish and what forms of communal life it can foster is to become interested in science. Such an awareness is not a modern province. The philosophical art was born from it in ancient Greece. But in modern times with the multiplication of communication media and the greater intensity of words, the loss of innocence is more serious, and, one might add, more widespread. Modern education, if it is successful at all, teaches one a variety of languages and makes him extremely sensitive to the functions of each one. A veritable war is waged on unconscious rhetoric.

Behind this growth of science in the modern world lies the kind of historical understanding which had its birth in the Renaissance and came to fruition in the Enlightenment. In this one learns to assess literature and speech in its own context, asking about the intention of the author, the means available in word and argument for him to make a point, the real significance of what he is saying, and the place of this work in the history that follows. No less than the meaning of a text depends upon such analysis.

Historical analysis means for the theologian not only the critical examination of the major texts of the Christian tradition — especially the Bible; it means also the loss of innocence surrounding the place of rhetoric in the church. Although the former has been rather clearly perceived for many years, the latter has never found adequate expression in theology. Thus the full implications of science have not been drawn. This is true despite the claims in many circles that theology is a science, because these circles are still seeing science as the skillful exercise of legal exegesis.

The shape of the theological task is greatly affected by the gradual debasing of the coin of rhetoric in the modern world. In certain cultures this has happened gradually, and we shall have cause to look at the German scene presently. In America it has happened more recently and a little more rapidly. Thus in the last century — and especially the last sixty years — the critical examination not only of the Bible but of the speech of preachers and churchmen has seriously called in question the rhetorical art. How well this is known in the churches is an interesting question; surely rhetoric in large areas of the populace can work remarkable things. For there is a lot of innocence around. But when it is lost, it can never again be attained without a *sacrificium intellectus.*

Theology is not what it was in classical times, for it has been caught up in the currents of the Reformation, the Renaissance, and the independence of science called Enlightenment. What it is now to be is open to question and depends in large measure upon its place within Christian religion. Reformation in theology, in other words, is not complete but has only begun. Herrmann saw this to be the outcome of Luther's experience of faith. The problem remains, however, as to how one since then outlines the shape of the theological task.

CHAPTER FIVE

Schleiermacher and a
New Reformation in Theology

IF THERE IS ANYTHING such as the Christian religion, thought Herrmann, it exists where the inner life of Jesus is kept alive in the community of faith. Here men are called to full self-possession and are disposed to moral action in freedom and responsibility. The inner life of Jesus is alive as traditions that derive from his own day and from Hebrew life before it give to the community a common past and refresh its life with a sense of the immediate importance of every moment when one speaks of God and the demands he makes upon men.

It is not the Biblical tradition alone which is with the church and informs the life of the community of faith. Also in this heritage are the many attempts in centuries of church life to express the experience of faith to other men so that faith may be born anew. For moral action among men presupposes some sort of communication and is completed only as others in their individuality are called to respond for themselves and participate in the new moments of history. Thus are built up traditions of past expressions of faith which help further new expressions of faith. Preserved as they are made articulate and available to memory and understanding, these traditions are valuable agents of continuity passing along the impulses that derive from Jesus.

Traditionalism is not necessarily the proper attitude toward tradition, and this is what Herrmann is attacking when he mounts his criticism of orthodoxy. For rather than serving with, tradition in this manner becomes the lord of faith and threatens its very life. At stake is the heart of the Christian religion itself.

Although traditionalism, labeled here " orthodoxy," was Herrmann's prime target in attacking an inadequate theology based upon an inadequate view of faith, rationalism was no less in his sights. In fact, it could be called a more serious threat to faith, since it had a ring of currency to it and could stake a claim upon modernity. Herrmann saw rationalism in every attempt to detach faith from orthodox dogma while leaving it attached to doctrine. Faith, although not being obedient response to an external and alien authority, was nevertheless response to a certain type of instruction and understanding supported by independent reasoning. But even in this form, faith was radically distorted. For the kind of trust and confidence that arises in the context of personal self-realization and is integral to one's relationship to the future he shares with others is done slight honor by being directed toward doctrinal statements even if these do not sound traditional.

Herrmann understood rationalism to do the same sort of violence to faith as orthodoxy, despite its freedom from ecclesiastical structures. In fact, one can say that it does greater violence, since it makes a pretense of freedom while yet vowing allegiance to other authorities active in other structures. Thus while offering a man a faith that claims for him an independence of judgment, the rationalist is really offering him a chance to commit himself to a different context of meaning and a different community that sanctions his actions.

In terms of Reformation thought, Herrmann found this making faith into a work.[1] Although the work might not appeal to the church for approval, it does appeal to a community of men who find themselves " learned " or " intelligent " or " enlightened " or " sophisticated " or what have you. For arguments of all kinds and the reasoning processes used in them not only arise in a particular historical context and are heir to customs and traditions appropriate to them but they also appeal to a certain community of men who find them convincing or unconvincing and give or withhold sanction backed up by social, economic, and political force.

We have already had cause to look at the effect of educational systems and their organization upon the unfolding of Christian teaching and the work of theology. In passing, we noted the relationship between theology and philosophy and the importance of understanding the place of the theological faculty in the life of the university for understanding the conception of philosophical work. In what Herrmann referred to as rationalism, new things are presupposed in the world that surrounds the intellectual life. The rise of sectarian struggles and educational instrumentalities organized to support one side or another had caught the university in its grasp in certain areas and eclipsed it in others. The spirit of modern science based on a revised view of nature and manifesting indifference to the sanction of traditional authorities often flourished outside the university or school and came to great currency in court life or in the salon culture of the eighteenth century. In addition the increased importance of the nation-state, the formation of national bureaucracies around the dynastic rulers, and technical and economic change all gave rise to various circles of men who responded to the claims of human reason and were convinced by its autonomous pretensions.

Although I mean to cast no aspersions upon the exercise of human reason and wish really to acknowledge indebtedness to those who in the pattern of truly educated men in all times have called the traditional in question in striving for the authentic, I want still to emphasize that no appeal to human reason is complete which does not acknowledge for itself that part of its reasonableness is found in its acceptability to a certain constituency.

Rationalism in theology seeks to undergird certain doctrines with convincing argument and in fact just selects facets of the classical orthodox Christian understanding of God, man, and the world and puts them together in a reasonable picture. In the seventeenth and eighteenth centuries the selection process could be generous and orthodoxy and rationalism could join forces. Some odd descendants of this marriage are to be found even today. If the selection process involved rather more critical use of the new notions of nature and was apprised of some of the implications of the scientific spirit, then a new rational structure was erected which could display creative genius and striking originality. It also could seem to live in a freer air intellectually. However, from the point of view of being fair to faith in its Herrmannian sense, this is still rationalism and is still beset with the weakness that attributes to faith a character which is wholly alien.

On the soil of Protestantism, rationalism may be doubly defective. For should it seek to support revelation — now seen in the word of the Bible — or seek to command belief outside of revelation, it still is declaring independence for a second time from the traditional without seeing that it operates in the sphere of the traditional when it comes to faith. What this might imply about the traditional itself must finally concern us, but what it does to faith and the Christian religion along with it is of more immediate interest.

The flourishing of rationalism in the Protestant theological world is the immediate background of the work of Schleiermacher. In German culture this did not indicate as much alienation from orthodoxy as it might have in England or France, and, therefore, formal theological instruction, labors in philosophy, and pronouncements within the church might all have shared convictions and contributed to each other. The state tended to look to an orthodox consensus in its order. Schleiermacher raises only one voice among many in the critical analysis of rationalism. It is his, however, which renews the world of theology, for it is he who takes stock of the real implications of Luther's experience of faith for the theological task (even though he probably never took full stock of Luther!).

THE ESSENCE OF RELIGION AND THE THEOLOGICAL TASK

The forces that produced rationalism in theology also resulted in the tendency to treat religion as doctrine and to stop asking the question about true religion as the question about proper piety. When entangled in the web of orthodoxy, this tendency could drive men to argue about natural and revealed religion. When released from this web, natural religion would defend its independent existence, even though the real issue centering around how natural man might handle religion now that he came to examine it apart from an authoritative tradition remained obscure. Some consciousness of these issues arose in the critical thought of Hume and Kant, but the result was a chastening of religion within proper boundaries established by reason alone.

The general reaction to rationalism which was a feature of Romanticism in Germany found specific form in Schleiermacher's treatment of religion. Taking his place in the salon of Henrietta Herz, Schleiermacher sought to argue that religion is neither knowing nor doing but a fundamental awareness of one's individuality which comes as one is conscious of a unity in the world. This argument is directed to his friends and is in large measure an attempt to show them why he finds their company so much to his liking. Although they may appear to be the " cultured despisers " of religion, they are in fact voices in the wilderness preparing a way for God correctly understood.

Schleiermacher's important *Speeches on Religion* are a fulfillment of his calling. He is a preacher who, although seemingly alone in the circle of Romantics, is in fact at one with them. For they take very seriously the relationship between self-understanding and verbal expression. They know that individuality arising in the particular circumstances of one's own history reveals itself in the novelty of human speech and writing. Thus they know what it means to be religious, and they have encouraged Schleiermacher's religiousness. To be sure, for him this means a favorable reaction to the traditions of Christendom in which he has been raised and nurtured. But his task as a spokesman for these traditions now can be correctly seen only when his speaking fosters religion itself. The witness of the past is alive in the mouth of the preacher only when he brings it into the individuality of his own self-expression, not to coerce another into accepting it as doctrinal truth, but to invite another to the self-expression that will reveal anew the religious life.

So, Schleiermacher argues, religious life produces religious communities and within these communities there is an alternation of the common idiom in which they together find religion expressed with the peculiar declarations revealing that individuality of community members without which there is no religion at all. This alternation gives rise to the passing along of common creeds and philosophies which are yet appropriated only as they are newly understood and therefore contemporary. Types of behavior also become customary, but they are important for religion only as they come from the personal awareness of one's selfhood in a unified world.

By this means Schleiermacher bridged the gap between his place in the church as an ordained preacher and his place in the Romantic salon as litterateur. In both he was bringing his own individuality to expression — the one more traditionally and the other more artistically. But such was his calling and in fulfilling it he was being most religious. He was also significantly shaping the theological task, for in him come together several strains which we have laid out in earlier chapters and which now are integrated in a unique way.

Schleiermacher is a sensitive humanist. Whether it is as the translator of Plato into German, or as the man of letters in Berlin, or as the scholar-servant of the church, he has great sensitivity for the way an individual makes himself available in the style and content of his writing. For him literature is always reflective of a man who stands in a particular moment of history with a world appropriate to his self-awareness. Another man who engages in conversation with him by virtue of this literature does so as one who also stands in a particular moment of history and has his own world. Communication is effected in the community of humanity that exists by virtue of the richness of individual self-expression.

As a humanist Schleiermacher has a sense of the importance of historical context not only for the types of literature but for all the forms of self-expression. He singles out knowing and doing especially in his treatment of religion as being mediate forms of human life, reflecting clearly the historical medium that surrounds a man. They are contrasted to feeling as the immediate awareness of a man in his world, and feeling is thus seen to be a clue to the nature of religion. In viewing religion, therefore, one can never detach it from the medium in which it occurs and he must look at this medium with historical understanding both to appreciate the religion expressed and to avoid mistaking religion's real nature.

In this manner Schleiermacher released the idea of religion from the rationalist's grasp. He picks up the theme, which had been obscured by orthodoxy, of man's proper piety and raises the question most clearly of what is essentially involved in devotion and the traditional acts associated with it. The effect of this is considerable, for it gives rise to a variety of ways of approaching religion reflected, for example, quite differently in the scholarly pursuit of *Religionswissenschaft* and in the schools of Roman Catholic thought in Germany in the nineteenth century which sought a nonscholastic way for dealing with the richness of this tradition.

Posing again the problem of the nature of religion and its essence put Schleiermacher also in the tradition of Augustinian thought fostered by Luther. Although Schleiermacher himself did not identify closely with the great Reformer and in fact paid some service to his Calvinist heritage instead, he shares Luther's awareness that true piety is found only when one faces the peculiarity of his own being. He might paraphrase Luther's claim that " one must do his own believing just as he must do his own dying " with the claim that one comes to religion only as he fulfills his own calling.

Schleiermacher's calling, in a slightly different but related sense of the word, was as a professor of theology. In the new University of Berlin he lectured on systematic theology among other topics while continuing as a successful preacher in the Trinity Church. Thus he was forced to come to terms with the place of the university in the life of theology, and being endowed with remarkable systematic gifts, he did so in a highly significant way. Although uniting in himself the different activities of the preacher, professor, and man of letters, he was nevertheless able to draw distinctions between them and analyze the function that they served in the Christian religion.

As a professor Schleiermacher entered into a university tradition that had developed rather consistently from the time of the Reformation to achieve a certain independence of action and spirit now fostered by all the great universities of the world.[2] Before any others the German universities had adopted the critical spirit deriving from the Renaissance and coming to fruition in the eighteenth century and integrated it into the institutions of higher learning. The final success of German universities in the nineteenth century and their decisive effect upon higher education in general is well known. Schleiermacher at the beginning of this century was conscious of the demands of the critical spirit and took full stock of them in his dealing with theology as a science — in the proper sense of that word.

Theology as a science must fulfill two demands. The one, deriving from its place in the university and the canons of intelligibility which prevail there, is that its parts be connected into a whole. The other, deriving from the historical character of religion, is that it must bear constructive relationship to the church. Neither of these demands can be neglected or theology will be transformed into a purely academic enterprise like philosophy of religion on the one hand and render the theologian merely a clergyman on the other. When both demands are met, the theologian will take his place with other scientists in the academic community but will also contribute significantly to the guidance of the church.

Such a position is clearly in tune with Schleiermacher's understanding of religion. The theologian must be true to his individuality and this involves the skills and art of scientific thought. But he will not come to terms with his subject matter if he does not make serious connection with the communities of men where the traditions he wishes to put in some sort of order are kept alive. In these communities he serves not as the clergyman in preaching and rehearsing the common idiom, but he guides through his learning the understanding of these traditions and the use to which they are put. Even Schleiermacher's work as both preacher and theologian to say nothing of his life with the " cultured despisers " did not allow him to neglect this important distinction.

Within theology itself the balance between the systematic ordering of ideas and the historical production of particular forms of expression might be variously struck.[3] Thus one runs from philosophical theology at one end of the spectrum through historical theology to practical theology. At the beginning one appears to be asking the more theoretical question, although this is done in relationship to religion and especially Christianity as a religion. At the end one appears to be asking more about polity and program, although this is done in connection with the analysis of man's religiousness which is to be thus concretely expressed.

Between the two extremes is historical theology, including the disciplines that are more or less customary in schools of theological learning: Biblical studies, church history, dogmatics, and church and society. In every case Schleiermacher is quick to assert that the historical side of the question must never dominate the theological. Thus Biblical studies can never remain just philological and archaeological but must also raise questions of canon and hermeneutics to show the place of the Bible in the life of the church. Church history, similarly, must not become merely chronicle or general history but must foster reflection upon the characteristic energy of Christianity.

The place of dogmatic theology under the rubric of historical theology may appear strange to some and horrible to the Barthians, but it is grouped with " ecclesiastical statistics " (or what I have called " church and society ") as dealing with the present condition of Christianity. In this place it bears the burden of wrestling with orthodoxy and heresy. The former fosters

continuity in the Christian community and the dogmatic theologian must try to take stock of it. The latter recognizes diversity in the expression of faith, and both its divisive and creative potential must be evaluated. Since Christendom is not now
unified, the dogmatic theologian must also come to terms with
the antagonism that separates Protestant and Roman Catholic.

His remarks about the place of dogmatic theology in the
curriculum of theological studies is of great significance, for it
is that more than anything else which Schleiermacher practiced
as a university professor and it is that for which he is famous.
There should be no small wonder, then, that his great treatise
on *The Christian Faith* should take shape in the way it does.
On the one hand, Schleiermacher labored long and hard on the
architecture of his system so that it might be as coherent as
possible. On the other hand, he reflected at every point upon
the fact that his expression of theological concepts stood in direct relationship to his own piety and the piety of the community in which he found his place.

To make this clear he begins his dogmatics with propositions
borrowed from ethics, philosophy of religion, and apologetics.
In his specialized terminology this means that he adopts certain
theories from the science which seeks to study and interpret the
history of culture in order to clarify the nature of the church
as a religious institution. From that science which looks at
man's religiousness in its general sense to try to come to terms
with the diversity in religious communities he erects a scheme
for understanding monotheism and the historical center of living religions. The propositions borrowed from apologetics pinpoint the peculiar nature of the Christian religion in relation to
religion in general, the particular historical importance of Jesus
of Nazareth, and Judaism.[4]

Amid these propositions one finds the famous definition of
religion as the feeling of absolute dependence and the description of Christianity as a monotheistic religion of the teleological
type which is distinguished from other faiths of the same type
in that all things are related to the redemption which is in Jesus

of Nazareth. There are conclusions which derive from these propositions as well. Theology becomes a descriptive science of the doctrines that prevail in a given time and place in the church, and doctrines are conceived to be the Christian religious affections set forth in speech. The scientific task is fulfilled when these doctrines are ordered coherently, but of course this ordering process has already begun with the choice of propositions borrowed from the other sciences.

The system of doctrine itself unfolds in such a way that both the universal character of Christian religious affections and the specific historical context of their expression are kept in mind. Thus the first part, which deals with creation, the general attributes of God, and the perfection of the world, is based upon the presupposition for Christian religiousness. The second and by far the larger part, dealing with the more specific expressions of Christian doctrine such as sin and atonement, the person and work of Christ, the perfection of man, the church, and so forth, devotes itself to the expression of Christian religiousness in the antithesis of sin and grace. This is in turn the expression within the church of how the individual comes to the awareness of his own integrity over against and yet as a part of the universe. It is not ultimately to be distinguished from the realization of human selfhood in relationship to one's world.

TRADITION AND CRITICISM

Schleiermacher's breaking out of the circle of rationalism in order to deal with the Christian religion not as doctrine but as the expression of religious experience in the Christian community led to a greater appreciation of classical doctrine. His dogmatics is full of references to the great teachings of the church, and he is able to address himself both sympathetically and critically to the issues that have concerned theologians through the years. By virtue of his conception of theology as descriptive of Christian doctrines that prevail in a given time and place he is able to approach ancient dogmatic declarations in their own context and yet comment critically upon their applicability today.

This work of Schleiermacher was a work of renewal, and it is little wonder that he could be embraced by conservative theologians, by revolutionary ones, and by an important but eclipsed school of nineteenth-century Roman Catholics. Affinities with the work of Jonathan Edwards, who also reacted against the rationalism of the eighteenth century, have been pointed out.[5] In all, Schleiermacher could well have seen the effect of his emphasis upon the contribution of various individual self-consciousnesses to the wholeness of the universe.

However, Schleiermacher's treatment of tradition in the context of historical consciousness brings to the surface and into scientific discourse the attitude toward tradition which is implicit in Luther's faith. Traditional doctrine is not binding by virtue of being the ground of faith. It is informative by virtue of being the expression of faith. Thus it is not to be dealt with in a quasi-legal way as was the custom in theology. It is to be dealt with critically as is now the custom in science.

The Bible falls in the category of tradition. It too must be subjected not only to the critical dissection of philologists and literary critics but also to the critical scrutiny of the theologian. It becomes another, albeit the original, expression of faith which is intelligible only by means of historical understanding and relevant only when the faith expressed in it aids in bringing to existence faith today. Schleiermacher was shrewd enough to see two things: first of all, that Protestantism in its Scriptural principle was really only asserting that one comes to the church through Christ and not the reverse; secondly, he saw that in fact the doctrine of the church in various eras was not really very Biblical and reflected Biblical faith only in the same way contemporary preaching does. Thus, like tradition in general, the Bible could not be thought of as authoritative in the sense it had in classical Protestantism or in the church at large up until the modern period.

The import of the critical spirit is certainly known to anyone who occupies himself with theological labor. The boldness of Schleiermacher in acknowledging this and in setting about the task of theology fully aware of the radical departure he was making is not always recognized. With him theology is drastically reshaped and the theological task is drastically altered. Herrmann felt that this was a completion of Luther's reformation in which the intellectual consequences of rediscovery of the Pauline notion of faith were finally worked out.

Perhaps this reformation was even more extensive than Herrmann recognized. For not only is tradition exposed to the examining eye of the critical thinker; so also is religion. Piety is no longer that which is presumed by all to be valuable but is scrutinized to determine its nature and worth. Thus is completed what Smith calls the reification of religion.[6]

Piety or religion becomes something in the experience of man that can be looked to as an object of study. Although it is no longer conceived of as just doctrine, it is still, subsequent to Schleiermacher, thought to be something distinct in man's experience which has an identity of its own separate from philosophy, politics, and the like. Thus is founded the science of religion. And since the beginning of the nineteenth century, if indeed not earlier, the quest has been on for discovering the essence of religion.

It is not my interest now to assess all the various ways that religion has been subjected to critical analysis and the various judgments of value made about it. I wish only to indicate clearly that like the traditions of the church which were generally presupposed to be of value because they were brought to the common life by an institution acknowledged by all to be important to it, so also the practice of religion was assumed to be of value just because it was customary and woven into the fabric of the common life.

The critical attacks upon religion in the Enlightenment in general failed because they were really critical attacks upon dogma or traditional doctrine in the church thought by the orthodox to be the content of revelation. Schleiermacher and many following him could easily outflank this sort of attack just by doing their homework on the history of the church and the place of theological statements in its life. Kierkegaard is perhaps as interesting an example as any of this, and one can perhaps claim that his popularity in recent times has been more significant against the background of eighteenth-century legacies than in the contemporary scene.

The question Schleiermacher does not seem to have asked himself, however, is whether his focusing upon the question of religion and its essence does not so lift this into scientific view that traditional religion may never again be for the educated man traditionally conceived. To be sure, it may be argued that Schleiermacher's own view of religion, especially as this is articulated in close connection with his ideas of human individuality, necessitated breaking the ground scientifically for one's own individual constructions. Just as no absolute expression of doctrine could be conceived of as definitive of the Christian faith so also no absolute conception of religion could do justice to the phenomenon of religion.

However, Schleiermacher lived in a time when men were willing to acknowledge that piety was customary and that religion was woven into the fabric of their lives. Schleiermacher's true descendants are those ever since who have sought to argue for the essential place of religion in the lives of men even though the substance of traditional religion may no longer have relevance. But the black sheep among his heirs have refused to handle the topic of religion with the question of its value for human culture prejudged. They have, in most cases, been burdened with other prejudices which frustrate their critical labors, but to point these out is not to discredit their boldness in applying the tool of scientific thought to the sacred.

Schleiermacher seemed to have no fear of those who would pursue the study of religion in detachment from the church. What he called ethics and philosophy of religion and what developed into psychological, sociological, and anthropological research on the phenomena of piety and religious communities he saw as valid within the university but not at odds fundamentally with the work of the theologian engaged in church guidance. They were expressing their individuality in the exercise of their intellectual powers, and this could not but be of help to the theologian, even though he would reflect their insights within his particular endeavors.

One may not wish to argue with this view of the university and intellectual activity. But one should grant that this perspective comes from Schleiermacher's particular Chrisitan faith in which the various individual parts of the human community contribute through their individuality to the whole, and one in encounter with them has his sense of universality so heightened that he comes to what is called " the feeling of absolute dependence." Then in the face of scientific men who challenge this vision, he will either have to impugn their science or translate Schleiermacher's unitary vision to an eschatological dimension. In either case, the source of the vision would be brought more clearly forward.

With that the groundwork is laid for a philosophy of religion which with close reference to its historical development actually turns the moment of religious awareness into a moment of self-consciousness and self-understanding. The connection to customary piety and traditional religiousness is merely the connection of historical continuity which may be severed once one has drawn from it the illumination of his own experience. What has happened within the framework of a larger conception of religion and with greater sensitivity to history is a repetition of the rationalism of Kant in *Religionsphilosophie*. The line runs from Hegel to the Neo-Kantians, to Troeltsch, and to Pannenberg.

Herrmann sensed this deficiency in Schleiermacher's approach to the problem, even though he wished always to say that Schleiermacher had followed through in systematic theology the implications of Luther's understanding of faith and the great Reformation doctrine of justification. What Schleiermacher had not come to terms with was the Scriptural principle.

This, of course, leads to a very difficult problem. How does one do justice to the Scriptural principle without resorting to traditionalism albeit of a specific sort? Where is the way out of orthodoxy to be found in the desire to avoid rationalism? Is a conception of tradition possible which is not merely *religionsphilosophisch?*

Although these questions must be taken up later, it is important to note that Herrmann saw Ritschl as the one theologian who had tried to cut through the deficiency in Schleiermacher's thought and by virtue of the Reformation doctrine of justification sought to establish again the action of grace in the revelation of God in Jesus Christ brought to one by the Bible. Ritschl did not succeed in this attempt, however, and for that reason takes his place as the last of the great Scholastics.[7] Identifying with the tradition of the Christ, he adapted it to his own particular place in history without accounting theologically for tradition itself. The latter must be done by anyone operating in the atmosphere of modern critical thought.

Although he did not perhaps see the full dimensions of the problem contained in tradition, Herrmann was fully aware of the place tradition had played in the Christian religion and how its function had religious implications which could not be ignored. He was, therefore, not fully satisfied with Schleiermacher's way of unfolding the description of religious affections which prevail in the church at a given time and in a given place. Somehow one had to see the source of these affections in the experience of God's revealing himself. And it is for these reasons that revelation finally appears in Herrmann's thought as the key to the nature of religion as faith.

THE DILEMMA OF THE THEOLOGICAL PROFESSOR

In the twilight of his career Herrmann wrote an extensive article on the present situation and task of evangelical dogmatics.[8] Among other things he had cause to address himself to Troeltsch and Schleiermacher. Moreover, he reiterated his position that theology cannot tolerate orthodoxy in the realm of doctrine and takes the occasion to lampoon those officials in the church hierarchy who forced subscription to creeds upon young candidates for the ministry. They are, he says, guilty of the greatest crime against religion, for instead of encouraging the sort of freedom that is both characteristic of faith and morality — the freedom involved in taking possession of oneself and disposing of one's history — they encourage untruthfulness. The candidate who is forced to subscribe to a creed for the reason of obedience is introduced into hypocrisy to say nothing of immorality.

In this article Herrmann goes on to deal with the problem of revelation, aware of the fact that the Christian religion as faith depends upon one's being called to his full selfhood in freedom by personal encounter with another free self. One's inner life is born from meeting the inner life of Jesus kept alive in the Christian community. And as one meets the person of Jesus in this community one meets that person who creates in us all the freedom of inner life — God the creator and revealer.

One must be careful, Herrmann notes, to deal with revelation in connection with living religion and not solely in connection with doctrine. But he must deal with it if he is to recognize the particular character of Christianity. And he must insist that at no time can the universal validity of revelation be demonstrated or argued for; it can be experienced only by each one for himself. Thus the theologian who deals with revelation must never allow his exposition to stray far from the sphere of religion itself.

As we have already seen, Herrmann himself demonstrated great sensitivity to this question and was able to retain in his teaching not only the atmosphere of truthfulness so necessary for religion to take place and for perception of the person of Jesus in the Biblical tradition but also was a sort of evangelist to his students, impressing them with the strength of his own faith and opening for them the resources of Christian theology.

This, however, should not cause us to avoid asking whether this is in general possible or whether the peculiar circumstances which surrounded Herrmann's classroom did not lend themselves to the creating of an evangelical setting. In short, is it indeed possible to presume that the theological professor can or should be a preacher?

In Herrmann's case this question does not really arise. He operated in a state that saw its own self-identity closely linked to the health of the church and therefore saw no reason why the state support of theological education in the university was in any way questionable. To be sure, the theological professor was no substitute for the preacher and men did not look to the university classroom as the place in which religion was primarily disseminated. Nevertheless, the common life formed a sort of unity in which the various institutions contributed in their particular ways to making men citizens of a Christian civilization.

Part of the passion of Herrmann's writings stems from his feeling of responsibility for the church and the semiofficial place in the church given him by his place in state-supported education as a theological professor. One can in fact say that what Schleiermacher is able to rationalize as unity in the common life of various individualities — with institutions having individualities also — Herrmann presupposed in his professional life. He did not, however, buy the rationalization that Schleiermacher had used and he comments at some length upon the way the various sciences do in fact grow increasingly apart by virtue of the special languages and techniques that arise out of their special problems. Herrmann knew that the vision of unity which Schleiermacher had was religiously grounded and not an intellectual necessity. Retaining a healthy Neo-Kantian suspicion, he resisted giving academic disciplines and the institutions that foster them the kind of individuality that is proper only to persons. The leftovers of a vision of unity, however, did surround Herrmann and help shape the theological task for him.

One finds a curious sort of parallel here to the weakness in his Christological position that we have already pointed out. He did in fact think that the New Testament sources might so reflect the inner life of Jesus to the inquiring man that revelation would indeed take place. This has brought upon him a host of critics who are troubled about the implications of this for the study of historical texts.[9] The validity of these criticisms rests upon the inferences drawn from this position — not, I think, by Herrmann himself — that this is a clue to a historical-critical method. Herrmann has not protected himself sufficiently against these inferences, however, by focusing clearly upon the setting in which one is exposed to the New Testament sources.

I do not mean here to draw another incorrect inference seen in the Barthians that the church is the only place in which the New Testament might reveal God in the inner life of Jesus. Rather do I wish to point clearly to the framework of human community that Herrmann saw as so essential to the living presence of Jesus. This community may be found in the church or in other various bodies in the common life which by virtue of their connection to the tradition that derives from Jesus realize his presence. It may even exist in the university where the theological professor works.

One might further want to insist that human community in all the richness surrounding it in the Christian tradition may be essential to learning and to free and creative inquiry. Therefore, he might argue that the university is not self-sufficient but is a peculiar sort of institution which has grown out of the common life with odd and tradition-bound procedures that are intertwined with its fostering of creative human intellection — to both its help and its detriment. But it is a big step beyond this sort of assertion to the claim that methods and procedure within this institution will reflect faith. Herrmann does not take this step, but he comes perilously close, and those who do not understand the notion of faith as clearly charge boldly on. What we must do is to stem this charge.

The Christological examination which is necessary at this point can be sketched out only in passing; so difficult a task deserves primary focus. It must be indicated, however, for it is behind Herrmann's critique of Schleiermacher. A starting point is the realization that peculiar to the Christian religion is the structural necessity of continuous reference to the documents of earliest tradition portraying the relationship between Jesus and faith as the new life his particular career stimulated in the church. This new life seems to be real only when it is seen to come from outside oneself in the particular history of Jesus. It, however, only arises where the tradition about Jesus bears close relationship to the concrete institutions of communal life. The sacramental or religious context for reading, speaking, hearing, and understanding must be such as to confront one adequately with the decision of faith.

No understanding of the Christian religion is possible unless this alternation between Jesus the man of the past and Jesus Christ Lord of the community and the Author of faith is fully accounted for. Part of such an account will be an adequate explanation of Christology. Part will be a sufficient analysis of Christian religiousness. Also entailed will be a knowledge of the history of the church in the context of the history of religion. And all will be included in a theology that goes beyond Schleiermacher's attempt merely to set forth in coherent order the doctrines that have arisen in a given time and place to explicate faith. For the possibility of faith's retaining its form and taking place in the future will be entertained.

Such a theology, however, does not necessarily give rise to faith. For the events of cultural history surrounding the life of the church have produced independent institutions that have developed their own traditions and cannot exist apart from them. One of these is the university in which the educational implications of the Renaissance ideas of learning have been worked out and in which methods of teaching and research have been passed on by one generation to the next for refinement and criticism. The university is not monolithic, and increasingly the methods of teaching and research, to say nothing of learning in its various departments, have diverged. The resulting clamor of voices is anything but harmonic, and this actually complicates the problem. For theology has taken its place, for better or for worse, in this institution. In so doing, it has become academic theology with a vengeance, and the contrast between science and rhetoric in its expressions becomes increasingly clear. One may wish to bemoan this fact, but he would have to be blind to deny it.

When one in academic theology reads and analyzes the New Testament sources, he will have to come to terms with what is presented about Jesus, the historical problems of the origin and development of this presentation, the growth of a religion in which the figure of Jesus plays a necessary role, and the social structures and ideologies which grow from Christian religious life. He may feel called also to try in some measure to share in this life in order to understand it. But he may or may not come to faith as Herrmann understood this and his coming or not coming to faith is, in the last analysis, irrelevant to his success in academic theology.

Realization of this fact is pressed upon one who follows the course of New Testament criticism since Herrmann in which the figure of Jesus is placed firmly in the age of the primitive church. To be sure, the heady aroma of hermeneutic often envelopes historical research, confusing faith and understanding, but if one can clear this away, it becomes increasingly clear that the lingering hopes Herrmann had in the power of the New Testament text to arouse faith have been shattered. Now, it is possible to work out more consistently his notion that faith has to do with the basic realization of self in human community. One can notice that the relationship of faith to academic life and intellection is multifaceted and ambiguous. And along with this he can make clear that no amount of sophistication can take the place of the demands of one's own history.

ACADEMIC THEOLOGY IN AMERICA

The cultural undergirding for Herrmann's work as a theological professor in Germany may once have existed in the United States, but it has been increasingly undercut. American educational institutions have developed in an atmosphere of voluntary religious bodies whose support from the state has been indirect. Theology has suffered its own sort of identity crisis in this setting.

In the beginning of American higher education the theological enterprise stood at the apex of instruction much as it had in the universities of the Reformation. The desire for a learned clergy in a state that was self-consciously of one confession or another led to the founding of colleges devoted to this purpose. One need not rehearse the tremendous influence of this notion and point out again the remarkable part the church took in founding the centers of higher learning in this country. Presupposed was the place of theology still conceived according to the pattern of the Reformation era as the exegesis of authoritative tradition — even when this tradition was thought to be completely Biblical.

The secularization of higher education in this country followed the secularization of the state, but it has operated according to the same principles. Therefore, a great suspicion of sectarian pronouncements by theologians is fostered in all the centers of higher learning no matter how conciliatory they may have now become to the scientific study of religion.

The response to this secularization has been various and unclear. In the first place, the consensus confession of faith worked out in the eighteenth century in reaction to extreme sectarianism and woven into the basic fabric of the American consciousness has been assumed by most citizens to be normative in schools and universities.[10] The recent realization that the high court of the land did not read the First Amendment in this fashion only brings to public consciousness the intelligence known to anyone conversant with the university that its faculties share the court's sentiment. Thus there is a general uneasiness abroad about the place of religion in the university and the need for more of it. Of course, religion is here understood in the fashion of the seventeenth and eighteenth centuries and faith is completely misconstrued as doctrine.

In the second place, the response by more narrowly confessional bodies represented by many of the denominations, although more sophisticated about faith, has been to establish special theological institutions of learning and look upon the university as the field for mission and ministry. I do not mean to impugn this instinct and I see ministry to the college and university campus as a valid expression of faith. But for theology this has most interesting ramifications. The seminary professor claims for himself the standards of the university, but by the constituency of his student body occupies himself with instruction for professional activity. If the seminary is attached to a university, the other faculty members know not how to look upon the theologian, especially if he as a member of a Christian community may aid in the mission to the university as a whole. The difficulty of communicating the distinction the theologian makes between his role as academician and as member of the body of Christ is heightened by the residual suspicion within the university of confessional proselytizing. The legacies of the seventeenth and eighteenth centuries still carry great weight. Furthermore, seminary curricula are not products of academic subject matter alone but are highly influenced by the ecclesiastical office that the student will soon occupy.

A third approach to the secularized university seems now to be less a possibility but commends it to many, especially within Roman Catholicism. This is to run competition to the secular university by refurbishing the private church-controlled school in which theology can be given its God-determined place. The financial and cultural obstacles to the success of this enterprise may be left out of account. The greatest objection of this from my perspective comes from the misunderstanding of the theological enterprise involved and the refusal on the part of church authorities to become detached from the era of orthodoxy and confessionalism.

Many who are sensitive to the rich legacy of the theological tradition, to the place of religion in human culture, and to the variety of intellectual needs in the contemporary university have sponsored the reentry of the study of religion into the university curriculum. Theology has in this way been smuggled in under the guise of philosophy of religion or " religious thought " or some other innocent-sounding euphemism. Schleiermacher can be the patron of this activity, since the description of doctrines that prevail in a given time and at a given place in coherent fashion seems to command adequate academic credentials. And one can feel, I think, that this is not a bad compromise given the circumstances.

However, what is done in this fashion is neither wholly honest intellectually nor helpful to the one who really wishes to make some sense for himself of the theological task. On the one hand, it seems to perpetuate the sort of misunderstanding of faith which comes out of orthodoxy and therefore to inhibit a forthright penetration of the meaning of the Christian religion. Since the latter has an undeniably important place in the history of Western man and the formation of his institutions, intellectual honesty should force one to understand it most accurately. On the other hand, the theologian is not forced to face with sufficient clarity the fact that he lives in a scientific world and must see his discipline in its light. Schleiermacher becomes then not the resting place but the beginning point for his serious reflection.

The result of clarifying the place of theology in the university is not peace and quiet. As a faculty member in good standing the theologian will come under the criticism of those outside the university who protest its secularity. He will be forced to communicate to the church the ambiguous position he is in and the compelling reasons he feels as *theologian* for adhering to the canons of the university. No doubt the more he wishes to take his place in the church and the more he feels responsibility to express his faith, the more wracking the tensions will become. The retreat to the scientific study of religion is an easier out.

This way out must not be taken, however, even though the scientific study of religion is a worthy academic endeavor. For the theologian bears some real responsibility for the adequate understanding of the whole intellectual tradition that has grown up around the church's attempt to express faith and talk about human existence in the world in faith. Furthermore, the university, if it has any sensitivity to its history and the part played by the Christian religion in shaping Western culture and the value systems within which we operate, needs the theologian at work in its midst. That he might help clarify the vexing problem of the relationship between church, state, and educational institution is a *donum superadditum*.

At this point I think we have reargued Herrmann's case with some additions sufficiently and translated it into the American scene. It is now necessary to see how his perspective might help us in sorting out the terms of the theological task today and how his contribution to this particular facet of Christian history has helped to give it its shape.

CHAPTER SIX

The New Shape of the Theological Task

PERHAPS IT IS NOT NECESSARY to have theology, but in fact we do. It has come into being as the Christian religion developed and has been deeply involved in the growth of education and learning. This alone might justify its right to exist today, even though many would contend that its place in higher learning has been preempted by other disciplines. However, that is not sufficient for the theologian, and I for one wish to argue that the work which goes on in other fields does not include all the relevant issues and the disciplines fostered there are not entirely adequate for the theological task.

This need not be said merely with respect to the fields of history, philosophy, sociology, and anthropology in which religion is considered. Nor does it apply only to disciplines such as philology and literary criticism as these are generally practiced. It applies equally well to those fields and disciplines worked under the general rubric of religion. The theologian borrows from those scholars who apply themselves to understanding Biblical text as well as from those who assess the nature of religious experience. He is engaged often himself in church history and the history of religions. But he continues to ask himself questions about how the tradition that has come to him out of the life of Christians can be responsibly handled. Furthermore, inasmuch as the Biblical scholar and the church historian, and certainly also the historian of religion, share in this feeling of responsibility for the traditions arising out of Judeo-Christian religious life, they share in the theological enterprise.

The whole purpose of this study has been to bring the theological task into closer focus so that we can assess its shape. It is not meant by this procedure to surrender theology to the science of religion nor to detach it from the university. Rather, I wish to show that the proper task of theology today can only be worked within the university and any other course will only lead to isolation and obscurantism. Moreover, I wish to claim the validity of theological method both within the canons of intellectual honesty and for the health of the Christian community. To make this point most clearly let us resume the argument.

Theology came into being as part of the process of men communicating to one another what it meant to be part of the community of faith. Faith as the trust and confidence of one whose style of life is determined by the coming of the new age in Jesus the Christ necessitated that one speak of the origins of this new life, its character, and its hope. And this speaking was itself an exercise of faith, since it reflected the fundamental disposition of the man who speaks in relationship to the one he addresses.

The connection between faith and its communication was given a most important expression in the Johannine picture of Christ in which the preaching of Jesus, the proclamation of the church, and the life of faith are drawn together. The trust and confidence that are so characteristic of the Christian life came to be seen as response to the kerygma of the church, and this in turn rests upon the concrete declaration of God's Word in Jesus. In faith comes the enlightenment that tells one of his true place in the world and the way he can occupy it most fruitfully. Thus does the revelation carried along by the church in its preaching partake of the divine action that saves men. The resulting knowledge that comes to one in faith from this revelation completes his incorporation into the life of the new age.

This Johannine provenance managed to gain dominance in the circles of the church which were trying to spell out the implications of Christian faith and bring it into some connection with the spiritual quest of Hellenistic men. Religious and intellectual claims were one as the Christian asserted that their specific revelation provided the way for human nature and human culture to find their perfection. Knowledge in all its forms would have its true context set only when men were properly illumined. And the quest for the divine as the key to the fundamental principle of all things could be fulfilled only as one came to know through the preaching and teaching of the church that God is Father, Son, and Holy Spirit as set forth in Jesus Christ. In this knowledge he found himself transferred from the realm of darkness into light and his moral sense sharpened.

The power of this synthesis of ideas in affecting the shape that education took in the centuries which make up the Christian era was very considerable. Thus intellectual history in the Western world is in large measure dependent upon the way rhetorical techniques, scientific methods, and literary modes were geared to the communication of Christian revelation and the developing of cultivated persons. In connection with the external events of history this tendency brings theology into full bloom in the medieval period and places it in a faculty of its own in the university.

This tendency helped also to bring into being a whole great body of literature centered around the Scriptures and the key and definitive assertions thought in some way to be closely related to revelation either in explicating it or in describing its limits. A tradition with authority over the community of faith defined an orthodoxy that was increasingly interlaced with subtleties of distinction. Brilliant as these exercises in human intellectual ingenuity were, they always stood in some real tension to the new life that faith originally designated.

The tension reached the breaking point with Luther when the emphasis upon faith in its Pauline dimensions brought about a challenge to the authority of the tradition and the agencies that supported it. Although this challenge was based upon the claim that the real origins of Christianity were being revived, and although the full implications within the exercise of theology to say nothing of the church were not worked out, the question about faith's true nature had been raised and the dominance of the Johannine provenance was threatened.

These events found a strange echo in the development of scientific thought through the period from the Italian Renaissance to the Enlightenment. Thus the place of theology in the university was challenged from two directions: from within in connection with the real relationship between faith and human intellectual life and from without by the increasing demand for cultural independence by Western men. Schleiermacher responded to these two challenges brilliantly by trying, on the one hand, to speak about the relationship between religion and science and, on the other hand, by trying to define a place for theology in the university responsible both to the community of learning and to the community of faith.

Herrmann in the footsteps of Schleiermacher saw him working out the implications of Luther's understanding of faith within the theological enterprise but was finally uneasy with the fact that the dimension of faith for which Luther had provided with his insistence upon the authority of Scripture was yet neglected. With this the door was opened for theology to pass over into philosophy of religion and the possibility was real that faith might disappear. In my terms this means that the place of original tradition in faith's coming to be is not sufficiently dealt with.

The place of theology in the university, however, was not fully accounted for. And the loyalty to both the community of faith and the community of learning found in Schleiermacher and Herrmann is increasingly difficult for us to uphold in a society whose pluralism calls in question the alliances of state, church, and university as these have prevailed in recent history. Although I mean in no way to say that statements and means of expression which appear within the church and serve most immediately the church's purposes are not relevant to theology, they certainly are not theological. They are, instead, part of the subject matter for the theologian who must find his place in the university abiding by the canons of scientific criticism and appealing to no authority outside of the free inquiry for truth. No coercive power from church or state can be brought to bear upon the theologian's work.

I make this point so strongly because I am convinced that the problem of tradition and the integrity of theology as a university enterprise are closely related. The course of history and the development of the Christian religion have brought them together, and until the problem of tradition is spelled out in such a way that it can be dealt with in a university setting, the new shape of the theological task will not be correctly outlined.

How to Deal with Tradition Untraditionally

To head off any premature criticism of my insistence upon placing theology in the university, let me say clearly that the university is not immune from the sorts of pressures that brought orthodoxy into being in the church. In fact, it has its own orthodoxies and its own forces of coercion which compromise so constantly the proclaimed ideals of truth. Nevertheless, it has become the agency in contemporary life in which the modern scientific spirit is nurtured and the critical sense fostered. Its attitude toward the traditions that men develop in the various institutions of society is one of examination and independent judgment. Although it does not perhaps bring its own institutions under enough scrutiny for its own good, it does nevertheless sow the seeds of its own rebellions.

For the theologian, this must mean at least three things. In the first place, the training men receive for the major professions, for technical work, and above all for educational activity is based, if it is successful, on the sort of critical analysis that refuses to look favorably upon the traditional just because it is traditional. Rather, it must always be suspect unless it can be brought into some sort of constructive relationship to present life and activity. To appeal to it in any other terms is to imply that an entirely different mind-set is necessary when one comes to the material of theology.

Some, no doubt, would like to make this assertion. However, it is fatal for the theological enterprise if one sees this in Herrmann's terms. It can also be argued that it really stands in stark contrast to theology's own history and tradition unless you find this history fulfilled in the era of strict confessionalism and encrusted orthodoxy. I think no one need listen very long to the cries for " relevance " or operate very long in the university setting to know that the first instincts which originally produced the theological enterprise are more genuine to the Christian religion than orthodoxy's vain attempt to defend a lost empire.

Thus it is of paramount importance to place theology in the university setting, where it must come to terms with modern critical thinking. Not the least important part of this experience is the incorporation of the historical-critical method into the theological enterprise in such a way that no theologian can avoid dealing with it. In fact, anyone who has theological training will know that this is now commonplace even to the point of making history and historical method one of the enduring issues of theological discussion. What is not sufficiently done is to make clear to those within the church who inform themselves of theological work and perhaps try their hand at it that these are the canons of operation and to disobey them is to compromise the integrity of the endeavor.

Placing his enterprise in the university means in the second place for the theologian that he must come to terms with the current questions of education. Since education involves bringing the legacy of the past into some sort of constructive relationship with the present, one is brought close to the heart of theology itself by asking how one in the present day can find authoritative something delivered to him by his ancestors. In the modern university the suspicion that was directed toward traditional material during the seventeenth and eighteenth centuries has become the commonplace. Everything is skeptically examined or education has passed over into mere training. On today's campus there is a healthy suspicion of training.

Herrmann was not far from understanding this dimension of the problem, for he brought faith into intimate connection with self-development and self-realization. As one in modern education thinks of learning in terms of self-realization, he presses to make sense of the same thing that interested Herrmann. Furthermore, Herrmann is a true humanist just as Luther was in essence a true humanist. The crux of the problem lies in the awareness shared by Luther and Herrmann that one comes to self-realization in a structure of grace. That is to say that self-realization is possible only in a community of selves in which mutual responsibility motivates all. The prominence of this idea in the educational enterprise may in large measure have resulted from the influence of Judeo-Christian religious life, but it now has an integrity of its own that in turn may enrich the tradition from which the original impulses came.

What I am saying in part is that the struggle not many years ago between religious educators and theologians needed better insight on education and more sensitive knowledge of the nature of theology. Then it might have been a struggle which produced important results rather than the occasion for lasting hostilities and abysmal lack of clarity.

Finally, from his place in the university the theologian may dispel any lingering hopes that a pluralistic society may pass away and the unity of church, state, and university may be restored. For there is present in the church a vestigial expectation that society will see it as important for the well-being of all and of greater importance among the institutions of man than those with other traditions and other histories. In fact, in this country and I daresay in others as well, the privileged place the church has had in human society since the time of

Constantine is lost to it forever. Increasingly the centers of power, influence, and originality are becoming diverse and increasingly men feel little need to call upon the church even for legitimization. The growing hostility toward actions by clergy and others in the church in attempting to touch the centers of power is evidence enough albeit indirect of the independent claims of the various members of our pluralistic culture.

In contact with the critical spirit of the university the theologian is in a better place than those who have executive responsibility in the church to remind them constantly that they must not presume upon the authority of the tradition given them. This happens not only by raising a critical voice about institutional organization and the social and political biases reflected in church actions. The role of social critic and gadfly is not especially appropriate for the theologian and is assumed by those who operate under the banner of theology or the study of religion no more logically than by those who do general social criticism. To be sure, since attention and interest are directed toward the church in these settings, a greater energy may go into this sort of work here than elsewhere.

The theologian himself, however, must attack directly the use of traditional ideas and traditional methods of expressing faith to find out if indeed they are not stifling faith. And at the heart of this critical examination of church life in the present day lies the problem of tradition itself. How indeed does one take hold of the Christian religion recognizing the place that the authority of tradition has had in it and transform the nature of this authority without finally destroying it?

Perhaps this can be most clearly illustrated in a look at the Bible. Almost until yesterday — and in certain circles even today — it has gone unquestioned that the Bible stands over the church and that it is reasonable to appeal to it in the interest of settling vexing questions. Involved in this assumption is the thought that it in fact must be relevant to present-day problems and all one needs is the methods of unlocking its secrets. Such thinking is no longer possible. Since the rise of historical-

critical analysis, men have been taught to challenge the under-
lying assumption. A similiar attitude is reflected toward laws
and constitutions; why cannot the churchman take stock of it
as has jurisprudence?

What I am not saying is that the Bible should be returned
to the past as a curio piece to be given its due when one tells
the story of Western history and its development. Nor do I
wish to look upon it only from the perspective of great literature. No theologian can overlook the fact that the use of the
Bible in the church has been all bound up with the very structure of the Christian religion and has been deeply related to
the reality of faith. Herrmann's awareness of this and clear
insight on its importance for the theological task has been noted.
What is needed beyond Herrmann is an evaluation of whether
one must not look for new ways of keeping the Bible alive in
connection with faith consonant with contemporary suspicion
of tradition for tradition's sake.

The implications of this way of looking at the Bible for the
preaching of the church, the nature of church education, and
even for the shape of liturgy are readily apparent. The present
practices of the church which in fact debase the coin of its
authority will come in for radical change. Perhaps some reshaping of the preaching and liturgical functions of the ministry will
follow which will be in tune with the growing pressure for
specialized clerical training and activity.

This is, however, not the important theological point. Rather,
the theologian will have to examine whole new schemes with
which to talk about the authority of Biblical text and with it
all the various sources which are carried in the memory and
literature of the church and condition its life. Furthermore, no
scheme will do which relies upon traditional ideas of revelation.
For these are in fact the outcome of faith's being conceived
according to the pattern of the Gospel of John — a pattern
that now can no longer be considered apart from critical-his-
torical examination of its tendencies and adequacy.

Interestingly enough, this problem transcends the confessional rifts arising from the Reformation of the sixteenth century. It has ecumenical dimensions which are striking, especially in this day when Roman Catholics and Protestants are discovering affinities in their use of and reverence for the Holy Scriptures. However, the ecumenical perspective here opened differs markedly from that reflected by many ecumenical discussions and declarations. For in these discussions it becomes painfully evident that neither Protestants nor Roman Catholics are properly sensitive to the fact that reduction of authoritative tradition to the Bible does not remove the problem of the authority of tradition. The danger is that we may have one fossil rather than two in the same rock. To avoid this danger some ecumenical theology is needed which is authentic to both terms.

When the Bible is looked at with the question of its authority open, then one comes close to seeing how it arose, what exigencies determined its form, what authentic motives may have been involved in its writing and preservation, what antiquities remain which have no real relevance to the present day beyond that, what terms and ways of thinking were drawn into the orbit of Hebraic and Christian communities to speak of their life and in that speaking to help create it, and finally, how new communities have arisen which find integral to their constitution this rich and varied heritage. And in the midst of these communities a form of human life has received definition which commends itself to all men without the intention of robbing them of their humanity.

Obviously, this is a theological judgment in the proper sense of the word. It depends upon the work of Herrmann, who isolates faith as the key to understanding what is continuous throughout the communities of men and can in broad terms be called the Christian religion. I, in standing upon Herrmann's shoulders, have tried not to leap out of my own skin but have sought to refine his notions in such a way as to indicate my inescapable dependence upon my own tradition and also to show that honesty to that tradition which makes so much of faith requires independence from it. Faith at present, largely because of its place in tradition, seems the best category for understanding the continuity of the Christian religion and also its ability, by means of constant reference to a primitive tradition that reflects the Lordship of Christ over his church, to criticize other traditions. Now, this primitive tradition itself must be scrutinized to see how faith has come into being or the true nature of its authority will be misunderstood.

What this does to the usual categories of theology will be immediately obvious to anyone who has tried it even a little bit. Then the literary form in which Herrmann cast his writings will command some real sympathy, and the variety of forms of expression actually adopted by recent theologians will seem not an apologetic device but an inescapable necessity. To argue at all about dogmatics and apologetics will seem hopelessly passé.

An illustration of this can be seen if one harks back to the discussions of Christology that we have already had. Herrmann sought to do justice to the impulse in faith itself which fostered Christological speculation and in the process gave his approval to the orthodox Trinitarian solution of Nicaea-Constantinople. But he took exception to the formulation of two-nature Christology determined finally at Chalcedon. The latter he thought not authentic to faith and including a real misunderstanding of the place of Jesus in the growth and development of the Christian religion. This is the sort of theological judgment which is made in present settings that requires some radical rethinking of theological categories. For it places the Christological issue into relationship with historical-critical observations, thoughts about what is continuous in Christian religious life, and the problem of speaking meaningfully today. What is not raised but what must come to us now is the question of the proper literary medium for bringing the Christological issue to expression now. That remains a pressing and important puzzle. Perhaps theological essays are in order, and if so, the present essay can contribute to this type of literature.

Exercises of this kind which conform to the new shape of the theological task and which make use of traditional material and authoritative literature from the past in ways now possible cannot be successful without consideration of the limits in which they operate. For the need to deal with the traditional untraditionally brings with it a need for clarity and honesty that becomes more and more difficult to meet. But meet it the theologian must, for without this clarity and honesty he not only compromises his place in the university but he also detaches himself from the very substance of his theological concern.

THE MORAL USE OF THEOLOGICAL LANGUAGE

The reification of religion is in part the result of the confessional wars of the sixteenth and seventeenth centuries, the reaction to these in rationalism and the further reaction to this in the *Religionsphilosophie* of the nineteenth century. But it is also the result of the growing independence of men in making judgments about the world in which they live. Religious life is subjected to scrutiny and in a certain measure desacralized. We have already indicated the impulses added to the growth of modern critical ideas by Luther, and in this way one can speak of the basis within faith for such an attitude.

The results of the reification of religion for the life of faith are only beginning to be seen clearly. To reify is in fact to desacralize, and desacralization is a shock to the whole body of practices that have grown up in the church and have been commonplace for even the most sophisticated Christians. It is this shock which one feels in the experience of Dietrich Bonhoeffer and his call for nonreligious interpretation of Biblical concepts. Part of his place in current theological thought is the result of a similar shock experienced by others. Suddenly the holiness associated with words, actions, hymns, prayers, and the like is gone and in its place is a sense of refined powers of perception and the opening of a vast spectrum of moral alternatives.

In a way, there is in the reification of religion a loss of innocence accompanied not by a sense of guilt but by a sense of possibility. Faith is now possible as well as necessary, and it is in this faith that one is justified. With it comes a sense of responsibility to detach faith from its desacralized shell. Although the price exacted from time-honored institutions for this act is extremely high, there is tremendous fervor to pay it.

Part of what is involved in the reification of religion contributing to desacralization in an important way is greater sensitivity to the types of language used in it. Thus we can now see rather clearly that various styles of speaking, various intentions, and a diversity of thought forms have been involved in the church's language from the very beginning. Furthermore, we can reflect upon the place of rhetoric in every age of church life in the communication of faith. But to make these observations is already to place rhetorical language in a new perspective and to transform it in some way. To focus upon something and look directly at the function it performs is to stand over it in a position of judgment. Judgment is a challenge to authority, and the rhetorical language of church life now stands under this challenge. Therefore, preaching, policy statements, confessional documents, study papers, and liturgical books, all can be assessed as to their use of rhetorical techniques and judged accordingly. This use might be adjudged fair and correct, but in the very act of so judging, its rhetorical value is diminished.

For the theologian, the devaluing of rhetorical language is reason for pause. Not only in his style of writing, but in the conceptions he uses and the terms that are brought to the fore he must guard against banking upon rhetoric. He must do this not only because he claims to take his place within the university and the canons of science but also because he feels morally responsible.

This is what is essentially involved in all the ruckus about " the death of God." Men are trying to say that it is immoral to use notions that no longer reflect the way a man aligns himself with his world. Furthermore, the immorality of this goes counter to the very nature of faith as this comes to be in and from Jesus of Nazareth. Unfortunately, however, this claim is made in language which is itself rhetorical and encourages rhetorical response. This obscures the fact that speech about God has involved all sorts of language forms and that clarity on the issue can only come when these forms are sorted out and soberly assessed.

Theologically, such an assessment depends not upon whether one can reinterpret the idea of God or whether older and inadequate impediments can be removed from it but upon whether the idea of God and expressions about him are essential to faith and whether if not, how they can be correctly excised. The results of such a decision may have certain consequences for the rhetoric of the church which must also be soberly considered. Again, faith seems the most adequate notion to me for the assessment of the problem.

When the problem is looked at in this fashion, one sees how threadbare the fabric woven by certain contemporary " theologians " is. They operate without much clarity about the nature of the theological task and certainly do not indicate how they stand in connection with the institutions of our culture such as the church and the university. They also do not sufficiently set the stage for the responsible examination of the structure of the Christian religion in which the notion of God plays such an important place in order to make truly theological judgments about it. All this can be said, even though they may have quite good instincts about the malaise which is abroad in religious life.

The moral use of theological language in our day requires the use of scientific criteria for judgment. These include the historical-critical method and the sober and independent judgment striven for by the educated man. Even though the means of argumentation he may use in arriving at and articulating these judgments presents grave difficulties for the thorough thinker, there can be no excuse for resorting to rhetoric when claiming to do theology. This is not to say that use of rhetoric is necessarily immoral everywhere; it is just to point out that it is immoral in theology. In the realm of preaching and the other communication media it may also be discredited, but assessment of this problem must depend in the theological world on the criterion of faith. Here one asks whether rhetorical arts can in any way pass on the inner life of Jesus as realized in the life of men of faith together.

Now, of course, we have made it possible to have some perspective on those in contemporary theology who would see the major theological problem to be one of hermeneutics. They, focusing upon the difficulty of understanding and communicating the Biblical text in the circle of the church and being aware that faith is real only if it involves the very existence of the man of faith, have tried to tie together the speaking and hearing that have played so important a part in historical Christianity and contemporary reflections upon the clue language may give to the unique character of human being. In spite of the lingering traces of a theology of the Word, this has led these theologians to serious consideration of the conceptions they use with an eye to being honest about the current shape of existence and being responsible to men in allowing them the integrity of self-understanding and realization. The manner of speaking which is involved has likewise been open to question albeit with little real critical analysis of the viability of preaching in the modern community of faith.

Purged of traces of a theology of the Word, the question of hermeneutics becomes part of the larger question of handling traditional notions responsibly — not only in order to make them relevant to contemporary human needs, but also in order to see the actual context in which they arose and the contribution in that context and since which they have made to furthering faith. To be sure, the peculiar characteristics of human language and communication come into play when discharging the theological task and adequate understanding of this phenomenon is not only appropriate but mandatory for the one who would be responsible.

Such sensitivity to the problem of communication and the

linguistic character of human being and such sensitivity to the problem of understanding things that come from a distant and strange past not only makes one suspicious of rhetoric, it also makes one conscious of the need for economy in using ideas and expressions. With this sensitivity, the theologian is chastened to avoid the careless use of terms and explanations which will introduce problems that are either irrelevant to faith or misleading. He is also humbled, so that he no longer reaches out to comprehend things in theology which may not be appropriate to faith in the present day.

It is this which is of profound significance in the hesitancy shown by many theologians to speak of God. The awareness that metaphysical claims are involved in this notion and that with these metaphysical claims are certain ideas that require comprehensive significance causes the theologian to shy from it. Neither cowardice nor undue skepticism is at the base of this caution. Rather, it is the realization that when one is called to self-possession in order to dispose of himself morally in his own history, it is immoral to claim for himself knowledge and authority beyond the limits that faith prescribes. These limits are determined by the freedom of other selves met in love and drawn in faith to their own self-possession and moral calling. If these selves are not to be coerced into a view of the world which may not be proper to them, they not only deserve the right to reject terms and ideas that seem to them improper; they also deserve not to be patronized by the unspoken assumption that when they have seen all of the picture, they will agree to the meaning and relevance of a comprehensive doctrine of God.

In connection with the process theologians of contemporary times this has some importance. In their endeavors I think I detect mixed motives. On the one hand, there seems to be the hope that with significant adjustments classical metaphysical ideas that have had a time-honored place in the theological enterprise may be updated and made an option for modern man. It is assumed that the traditional metaphysical quest is still legitimate, and that assumption may or may not be correct. It seems, however, to entail the attitude of defending the time-honored. On the other hand, there seems to be a sense of self-conscious modernity in the process theologians in which present-day views of the world are looked to to transform the metaphysical notions of the past in such a way that they can increasingly comprehend the new ideas that history produces. Here the assumption is found that men can and will have comprehensive schemes to understand all of reality but only if they involve the latest ideas.

Although I have more sympathy with the second motive than with the first, and although there is a spirit of openness in the process theologians that is not ever to be denied, I am still concerned that there may yet be a resistance to faith here which takes the immediacy out of history and neutralizes the real moral demands upon a person in his time for life. We have seen in Herrmann the view that metaphysics is always a threat to faith, and I think what he discerns here is correct. Even those ideas which try to take change seriously do not necessarily do justice to the mystery of historical life, and I have the distinct impression that this is really the subtlest form of *Religionsphilosophie*.[1] In connection with faith the doctrine of God must be protected from its metaphysical seducer.

Whether the doctrine of God is still of significance in the theological enterprise is, I believe, an open question. An answer to it, moreover, will be given only when one is clear about the theological task and aware that many other things are entailed, such as the nature of the Christian religion, the present setting in which words and concepts are communicated and received, and particular persons who seek to come to terms with their historical responsibility. Such awareness springs from and contributes to an understanding of how the notion of God has become such a pivotal idea in the history of Christianity and furthermore makes one conscious of the crucial step taken in its abandonment.

The moral use of theological language is a direct consequence of faith. It is also the way in which one can really be responsible for a tradition while not treating it traditionally. And it is absolutely necessary in the present age when men are ill-disposed to accept the authority of things past for the determination of things future. Furthermore, it grounds the only kind of apologetic which today is either reasonable or relevant. This is the defense against uneconomical and sloppy perpetuation of platitudes that neither deceive the educated nor move the ignorant. It flows from an intellectual austerity that takes seriously the power and significance of a man's ideas for the disposition of his world. No less than this is required for adequately discharging the theological task.

PROGNOSIS

If I have given perspective on theology in this essay by returning to Wilhelm Herrmann, rearguing his case, and updating it so as to outline today the shape of the theological task, and if this task today is to speak of traditional matters untraditionally as a faithful man called to moral responsibility for his history and the place of theological notions in it, then my work is almost complete. It would be remiss, however, to end without some indication where the future of theology may lie. With full knowledge that this is the most dangerous ground on which to tread and properly aware that the judgments which follow are theological in the best sense of the word, I will attempt some prognosis.

In the first place, theology in the university of today will find its techniques, methods, and basic concepts altered even more than is now imagined by interaction with other fields and disciplines. Aware properly of his task, the theologian will be searching for ways of understanding men and the world in which they live. Thus he will share with the sciences that focus upon human nature and society the quest for methods, data, and terms of evaluation that are proper to human life and sufficient to lend criteria for treating it responsibly. The theologian in this joint enterprise need be neither apologetic for his activities nor reduced to second-class status. He need not be embarrassed by the tradition that he brings with him or restrained in critical analysis of the traditional assumptions that sneak into every science. Nor does he need to surrender his ultimate aims in trying to clarify the expression of faith, for the goals of the educational process are his as well as they are the goals of others. Failure by the practitioners of other fields to recognize these goals is either part of the historical legacy their tradition bears or the hostility in separation which may be overcome in the reconciliation which is integral to faith.

As one of the sciences of man philosophical analysis has had in the past a special relationship to theology. Although this is probably a thing of the past, a word about it is appropriate here, for in the education of theological students and in the discussions of the theological community the place of philosophy is often considered. If I read correctly the tendencies of both European and Anglo-American philosophical work, then it is correct to say that theologians must learn to adapt this work to theirs in a rather different way. In both the schools of phenomenology and of linguistic analysis an enterprise is being taken up in which man is considered according to the inter-relationship of thought, consciousness, verbal expression, and logical order. Although the locus and extent of meaning is at issue between them, the linguistic analysts generally restricting it to a property of words and language, they are at one in avoiding cosmic claims for their ontology. Thus the means for connecting the philosophical and theological tasks used in the past have been destroyed. A new method for making use of philosophical analysis must be found by the theologian which takes account of its totality and understands it in some measure at least as anthropological.

Requisite to this use of philosophical material is the kind of clarity about the theological enterprise for which I have been arguing throughout this essay. Often it is this and not a lack of philosophical skill which causes confusion and misuse of philosophical tools. Especially is this the case in most of the writings which one finds devoted to using linguistic analysis for dealing with theological assertions. It is supposed that these assertions are the content of faith and hence they are subjected to the kind of scrutiny which is not really relevant to their actual historical occurrence.

It appears to me that actually reflections on ethics and law provide the richest source of philosophical material for the theologian. Both of these try in some measure to come to terms with traditional exercises drawn into the immediacy of present decision-making and the attribution of responsibility. Mining of these sources in the future may help the theologian deal with his particular tradition. He may as well lend insight upon the other traditions of our culture which have in such large measure drawn upon the ecclesiastical and religious resources of Christendom. Order then of the divergent strands of our pluralistic world may be facilitated.

Clearly, the theologian makes use of this philosophical material only along with the other sciences which occupy themselves with man. Another of them which stands out in importance is history. Now, from the beginning one must realize that history is a very diverse science and perhaps a " field encompassing field." [2] The techniques, means of argumentation, styles of writing, and the like are extremely different not only in various areas and in dealing with various topics but also in various historians. Careful analyses of these differences are about and can be fruitfully used by the theologian. But once again a cautionary sign must be raised which is not often noticed by theologians who concern themselves with history and historical science. The theologian must be clear about what his interest in history is, and this is in dealing with the scene of man's moral life in time and space. The scientific historian may in certain measure share these concerns, but his general procedures are usually dictated by the traditions of learning that he is heir to and the guild of craftsmen to which he belongs.

Because of the prominence of doctrines of revelation in theology and the connection to them of notions of faith according to the Johannine pattern, it is too easy to bring the question of history and historical method into the theological enterprise. We have seen some of the consequences of this in viewing Herrmann's descendants; in looking to the future we must insist that theologians see history with the other sciences of man, even though it may be the most difficult and may approach theology most closely in its attempt to understand the conditions for and nature of moral action. What must be avoided is the reification of history or a metaphysic of history built on hopes that the key to a unitary scheme of meaning may be found in Christian revelation. Such hopes are not only illusory, I think, but they arise from a misunderstanding of faith.[3]

The second thing that theology will experience in the future seems to me to be a growing state of tension with the organized church. This may go hand in hand with increasingly confusing ecclesiastical structures as the local parish unit experiences challenge by project- and task-oriented groups cutting across residential and denominational lines. At least, the theologian will increasingly feel discomfort in the church and may indeed find himself neither at home nor welcome. Moreover, he will see his theological insights implemented by other agencies in our pluralistic culture and will devote much of his nonprofessional energies to them. What is called " secularization " and means, when discharged of its more ethereal power, the passing over of functions played by the church into the tasks of non-ecclesiastical bodies will become an even larger factor. Instead of insisting upon a theological interpretation of history to justify his sympathy with this process, the theologian may just say that the tradition to which he is heir may be as authentically alive in other institutions of our culture as in the church. And he may find that this is the best way for the church to be called to the responsibility which is inherent in faith.

What this implies for the training of ministers and the place of theology in this is beyond the scope of this essay; however, some things are immediately apparent. Surely, with theology in the university and the theologian as much in other agencies as the church, the minister is bound to find himself in certain cases less well trained or capable in theology than many laymen and even than some who do not regularly participate in the church. If this staggers the imagination, it is only an indication of the very peculiar but interesting period of history in which we live. That it means some unknown redefinition of clerical functions, liturgical life, and ecclesiastical financing is no news to anyone.

As already indicated the way in which theology is written and presented to people will change with this changing relationship to the church. One will not be able to presuppose the same sorts of interests or questions in the reader and will have to approach his material with some greater attention to indicating why certain problems have been traditional in theology, why they may continue to be of interest, and how they may now be articulated. The prime concern is that faith find some expression in the lives of men.

Lest it be assumed that this means only innovation in theology, let me hasten to a final speculation on the future. I think that the theologian who has taken his place alongside the other students of human life in the university and removed himself emotionally as well as technically from a deep sense of responsibility for the church as institution will be able to discover riches which are hidden to others in the tradition that has arisen within Christianity as faith has been expressed and communicated. The interpretation of tradition untraditionally will mean the rebirth of things from the past. Unencumbered by the juridical mind the theologian will through historical understanding be able to raise classical issues in fresh perspective.

An example of this is in the whole complex of questions included in the Trinitarian controversies. Already Leslie Dewart had indicated the possibilities in Trinitarian notions for overcoming certain problems for contemporary man located in the doctrine of God.[4] An even more far-reaching analysis is necessary to evaluate all the attempts to bring together Hebraic loyalty to Yahweh in exclusion of other gods, Christian focus on the meaning of Jesus' Messiahship, Greek speculation about the divine, and the rich possibilities of life in the new age. It is not the resulting formula of orthodox Trinitarianism which is of interest. Rather, it is the process by which certain implications were disavowed, certain conclusions affirmed, and many problems never comprehended which enlightens the contemporary theologian. Thus instructed, the theologian may approach the current question of a doctrine of God with new tools and insights.[5] I daresay that this would be a fruitful starting place for most theologians today.

The term "liberal" as applied to Herrmann can now be given the proper shade. For what one means by this is a characterization of the attitude of openmindedness and freedom which motivated him. But this freedom was not freedom from the tradition but freedom for it. And with this attitude the theologian may probe with careful and steady hand into all the time-honored and explosive issues of the past to find what was at stake and what instruction for our present life in faith is offered. Liberalism in this vein is the only way for theology to go, but it is not a polemical ideology with set positions to be defended and an arsenal of weapons to be marshaled for attack.

Herrmann as the great German liberal is the point we selected for departure in this study. It becomes increasingly obvious that he may be this not only because one feels his influence so close upon oneself but also because his view of faith and the theological task can be adjusted to every new generation. His liberal spirit and sense of theological vocation can continue to live as other theologians sense their own calling to this task. And as this task is reshaped in the coming years the willingness to share in this process will be an expression of loyalty to Herrmann's insights.

Here we have come to the end. Perspective on the theological task need neither take us out of the tradition which helped produce us nor make us slaves to it. The structure of faith itself demands that one know the way his existence is given him and how in recognition of this he takes responsibility for it. The two come together in the exercise of self-possession and self-assertion in the course of history. Theology has come to be in the life of faith, taken certain shape in it, and will live in the future only as it is the work of faithful men.

Notes

Introduction

1. Most recently in the Braun-Gollwitzer exchanges about the meaning and significance of the idea of God, *Post Bultmann Locutum* (Hamburg-Bergstadt: Herbert Reich, 1965).

2. See the account of the *Zeitschrift für Theologie und Kirche* by James M. Robinson, "For Theology and the Church," *Journal for Theology and the Church*, Vol. I, ed. by Robert W. Funk with Gerhard Ebeling (Harper Torchbook, The Cloister Library; Harper & Row, Publishers, Inc., 1965), pp. 1–19.

3. Cf. "Translators' Foreword" to W. Herrmann, *Systematic Theology*, tr. by Nathaniel Micklem and Kenneth H. Saunders (London: George Allen & Unwin, Ltd., 1927). The following observation is of great interest also considering the source: "During the winter semester of 1905–06, I was a student at Marburg. Since I was intending to be a teacher of the New Testament, I confined myself for the most part to New Testament courses. But I did hear the lectures on systematic theology by W. Herrmann, and I have always rejoiced greatly that I had that privilege. In one's contact with any great movement, it has always seemed to me important to attend to its best, and not merely to its worst, representatives: and Herrmann certainly represented Ritschlianism at its best. He was a man, moreover, who could never fully be understood or appreciated through his books alone. Only personal contact could reveal the contagious earnestness, the deep religious feeling, of the man. I felt, as I sat in that class-room, that it was the centre of world-wide influence, a place from which a great current went forth, for good or ill, into the whole life of mankind" (J. Gresham Machen, "Christianity in Conflict," *Contemporary American Theology*, ed. by Vergilius Ferm [Round Table Press, 1932], p. 255).

4. Complete bibliographical information on Herrmann and his

interpreters is available in Peter Fischer-Appelt, *Metaphysik im Horizont der Theologie Wilhelm Herrmanns* (Munich: Chr. Kaiser Verlag, 1965). This work and the two articles by Theodor Mahlmann, "Das Axiom des Erlebnisses bei Wilhelm Herrmann," *Neue Zeitschrift für systematische Theologie,* Band 4 (1962), pp. 11–88, and "Philosophie der Religion bei Wilhelm Herrmann," *Neue Zeitschrift für systematische Theologie und Religionsphilosophie,* Band 6 (1964), pp. 70–107, are comprehensive contemporary attempts to revive Herrmannian insights.

CHAPTER ONE

1. The discussion that follows is drawn from W. Herrmann, *Die Religion im Verhältnis zum Welterkennen und zur Sittlichkeit* (Halle: Max Niemeyer, 1879).

2. "Warum bedarf unser Glaube geschichtlicher Tatsachen," *Gesammelte Aufsätze* (Tübingen: J. C. B. Mohr, 1923), pp. 214–238.

3. *Ibid.,* p. 220.

4. *Ibid.,* pp. 225–226.

5. *Die Religion,* p. 40.

6. *Ibid.,* p. 49.

7. *The Communion of the Christian with God,* tr. by J. Sandys Stanyon and R. W. Stewart (G. P. Putnam's Sons, 1906), p. 17.

8. *Ibid.,* pp. 33–34.

9. Cf. Wilhelm Pauck, *The Heritage of the Reformation,* rev. ed. (The Free Press of Glencoe, Inc., 1961), pp. 19–28. The subtitle of *The Communion of the Christian with God* is "Described on the Basis of Luther's Statements."

10. *The Communion of the Christian with God,* p. 72.

11. *Ibid.,* p. 73.

12. *Ibid.,* pp. 82–83.

13. "Die Busse des evangelischen Christen," *Gesammelte Aufsätze,* p. 33.

14. *Ethik,* 4th ed. (Tübingen: J. C. B. Mohr, 1909), p. 31.

15. *Ibid.,* p. 43.

16. *Ibid.,* p. 51.

17. *Systematic Theology,* p. 16. This book is made up of paragraphs used as the basis of Herrmann's lectures and was published after his death.

18. The argument appears in "The Moral Teachings of Jesus," tr. by G. M. Craik in Adolf von Harnack and Wilhelm Herrmann, *The Social Gospel* (G. P. Putnam's Sons, 1907), pp. 166–185.

19. *Systematic Theology,* p. 65.

20. *Ibid.*, p. 75.

21. *Ibid.*, pp. 139–145.

CHAPTER TWO

1. "Die Lage und Aufgabe der evangelischen Dogmatik in der Gegenwart," *Gesammelte Aufsätze*, p. 96.

2. Wilhelm Pauck, *Karl Barth* (Harper & Brothers, 1931), p. 20.

3. E.g., the presentation of the *Kirchenkampf* in Arthur C. Cochrane, *The Church's Confession Under Hitler* (The Westminster Press, 1962).

4. Cf. Braun, in *Post Bultmann Locutum*, Band I, p. 36.

5. It is especially evident in "Der Glaube an persönlichen Gott," *Zeitschrift für Theologie und Kirche*, Vol. XXIV (1914), pp. 21–32, 65–95.

6. This theme is developed at length in Barth's Gifford lectures, *The Knowledge of God and the Service of God* (London: Hodder & Stoughton, Ltd., 1938), Ch. 3, and in the *Church Dogmatics*, ed. and tr. by G. T. Thomson, G. W. Bromiley, T. F. Torrance, *et al.* (Charles Scribner's Sons, 1956 ff.), Vol II–1, Ch. 6. It is evident, however, already in his *Epistle to the Romans*.

7. Cf. the interpretation of Athanasius and Augustine in Charles N. Cochrane, *Christianity and Classical Culture* (Galaxy Book; Oxford University Press, 1957), esp. pp. 361 ff.

8. Karl Barth, "The Principles of Dogmatics according to Wilhelm Herrmann," *Theology and Church*, tr. by Louise Pettibone Smith (Harper & Row, Publishers, Inc., 1962), p. 244.

9. See his interesting remarks in the *Festschrift* prepared for his philosopher brother, "Philosophie und Theologie," *Philosophie und Christlicher Existenz*, ed. by Gerhard Huber (Basel: Verlag Helbing und Lichtenhahn, 1960), pp. 93–106.

10. *Theology and Church*, pp. 263 ff.

11. E.g., his doctrine of the "Royal Man" in *Church Dogmatics*, Vol. IV–2, pp. 154–264.

12. *Church Dogmatics*, Vol. IV–1, pp. 740–779. Here a play on words — *Anerkennen, Erkennen*, and *Bekennen* — forms the outline for his exposition of faith.

13. See "Die liberale Theologie und die jüngste theologische Bewegung," *Glauben und Verstehen* (Tübingen: J. C. B. Mohr, 1954), Vol. I, pp. 1–25.

14. *Jesus and the Word*, tr. by Louise Pettibone Smith and Erminie Huntress Lantero (Charles Scribner's Sons, 1934), pp. 218–219.

15. See his introduction to Adolf von Harnack, *What Is Christianity?* (Harper & Brothers, 1957), pp. vii–xviii.

16. Cf. James M. Robinson, "Kerygma and History," *The Bible in Modern Scholarship*, ed. by J. Philip Hyatt (Abingdon Press, 1966), pp. 114–150.

17. James M. Robinson, *A New Quest of the Historical Jesus* (Alec R. Allenson, Inc., 1959), p. 90.

18. *Ibid.*, p. 94.

19. *Ibid.*, p. 95.

20. Rudolf Bultmann, "The Primitive Christian Kerygma and the Historical Jesus," *The Historical Jesus and the Kerygmatic Christ*, ed. by Carl E. Braaten and Roy A. Harrisville (Abingdon Press, 1964), pp. 20–21.

21. T. A. Roberts, "Gospel Historicity: Some Philosophical Observations," *Religious Studies*, Vol. I, No. 2 (April, 1966), pp. 193–198.

22. "Einsicht und Glaube," *Theologische Literaturzeitung*, Vol. 88 (1963), No. 2, cols. 83–84.

23. *Ibid.*, col. 86.

24. Wolfhart Pannenberg (ed.), *Offenbarung als Geschichte* (Göttingen: Vandenhoeck und Ruprecht, 1961), pp. 91–114.

25. Pannenberg, "Hermeneutik und Universalgeschichte," *Zeitschrift für Theologie und Kirche*, Vol. 60 (1963), pp. 120–121.

26. *Offenbarung als Geschichte*, pp. 7–20, for reflections on current theologies of revelation.

CHAPTER THREE

1. See, for example, Helmut Koester, "GNOMAI DIAPHOROI," *Harvard Theological Review*, Vol. 58 (1965), pp. 279–318.

2. Extensive discussions of the word "faith" in the Bible are found in Rudolf Bultmann and Artur Weiser, "Faith," *Kittel's Bible Key Words*, Vol. 3, tr. and ed. by Dorothea M. Barton, P. R. Ackroyd, and A. E. Harvey (Harper & Brothers, 1960); and C. H. Dodd, *The Bible and the Greeks* (London: Hodder & Stoughton, Ltd., 1935). Cf. Gerhard Ebeling, *Word and Faith*, tr. by James W. Leitch (Fortress Press, 1963), pp. 201–246.

3. I have not departed here from the approach to Jesus' ministry outlined by Bultmann in *Jesus and the Word* and followed by Günther Bornkamm, *Jesus of Nazareth*, tr. by Irene and Fraser McLuskey with James M. Robinson (Harper & Brothers, 1961).

4. For a suggestive treatment of the resurrection, see Gerhard Ebeling, *The Nature of Faith*, tr. by Ronald Gregor Smith (Muhlenberg Press, 1961), pp. 58–71.

5. " Paul " is used here to include the apostle and " his school," if he indeed had one.

6. It seems to me interesting that Robinson, *A New Quest of the Historical Jesus,* does not hear the strong emphasis in Bultmann's presentation of Jesus' preaching upon the need for obedience, e.g., the quotation in the footnote, p. 42, and the use then made of it.

7. The question might arise in this context as to whether there is such a thing as " Biblical Theology." Certainly the work of Gerhard von Rad, for example, is done more nearly as history of Israel's traditions.

8. Werner W. Jaeger, *Theology and Humanism* (Marquette University Press, 1943), pp. 45–46, and *The Theology of the Early Greek Philosophers* (Oxford: Clarendon Press, 1947), pp. 1–17. Cf. Ferdinand Kattenbusch, " Die Entstehung einer christlichen Theologie," *Zeitschrift für Theologie und Kirche,* Vol. 38 (1930), pp. 161–205.

9. Notice that even here the term is " Christian philosophy." Kattenbusch, *loc. cit.,* p. 198.

10. Werner W. Jaeger, *Early Christianity and Greek Paideia* (Belknap Press, 1961), and Cochrane, *Christianity and Classical Culture,* Part III.

11. Interestingly enough, Justin used the word *theologein* to mean " allegorize." Kattenbusch, *loc. cit.,* p. 198.

12. Hugo Rahner, *Greek Myths and Christian Mystery,* tr. by Brian Battershaw (Harper & Row, Publishers, Inc., 1963), pp. 89–175.

13. See here Henri Marrou, *A History of Education in Antiquity,* tr. by George Lamb (Sheed & Ward, Inc., 1956), pp. 314–329.

14. David Knowles, *The Evolution of Medieval Thought* (Helicon Press, Inc., 1962), pp. 107–115.

15. *Ibid.,* p. 157.

16. *Theologia Summi Boni* and *Theologia Christiana* were titles of two of his works.

CHAPTER FOUR

1. *The Communion of the Christian with God,* p. 50.

2. *Ibid.,* p. 47.

3. On the relationship between Scholasticism and the Renaissance, see Paul Oskar Kristeller, *Renaissance Thought: The Classic, Scholastic, and Humanistic Strains* (Harper Torchbook, Harper & Row, Publishers, Inc., 1961), pp. 92–119.

4. *Ibid.,* pp. 8–11.

5. See Wilhelm Pauck's " General Introduction " to *Luther:*

Lectures on Romans (The Library of Christian Classics, Vol. **XV,** The Westminster Press, 1961), pp. xxiv–xxxiv.

6. Kristeller, *op. cit.,* pp. 8 ff.

7. Stephan D'Irsay, *Histoire des Universités* (Paris: Auguste Picard, 1933), Vol. II, pp. 305–330.

8. In this context the selection by Luther and others of the Lord's Prayer, the Ten Commandments, and the Creed for the focus of catechetical texts is interesting and indicative of norms by which Biblical text is to be used.

9. This is true no matter how one exegetes the famous " Scripture *and* tradition " of the Council of Trent.

10. Walter J. Ong, *Ramus: Method, and the Decay of Dialogue* (Harvard University Press, 1958), pp. 132–136.

11. Friedrich Paulsen, *The German Universities,* tr. by Edward Delavan Perry (Macmillan and Co., 1895), pp. 51–54.

12. John Dillenberger, *Protestant Thought and Natural Science* (Doubleday & Company, Inc., 1960), pp. 50–63.

13. One has to proceed in this matter somewhat more carefully, it seems to me, than Friedrich Gogarten, *The Reality of Faith: The Problem of Subjectivism in Theology,* tr. by Carl Michalson *et al.* (The Westminster Press, 1959), pp. 18–26, 85–97.

14. For what follows, see Ernst Cassirer, *The Philosophy of the Enlightenment,* tr. by Fritz C. A. Koelln and James P. Pettegrove (Beacon Press, 1955), pp. 37 ff.

15. Werner W. Jaeger, *Paideia: The Ideals of Greek Culture,* tr. by Gilbert Highet (Oxford University Press, 1945), Vol. I, pp. 286–298.

16. Wilfred Cantwell Smith, *The Meaning and End of Religion* (The Macmillan Company, 1962), pp. 15–50.

17. *Ibid.,* p. 37.

18. This distinction I take from Marrou, *op. cit.,* in which Isocrates the rhetorician and Plato the scientist are contrasted and the implications of each man's style for education are traced out.

CHAPTER FIVE

1. *Gesammelte Aufsätze,* pp. 104 ff.

2. Paulsen, *op. cit.*

3. For what follows, see Friedrich Schleiermacher, *A Brief Outline of the Study of Theology,* tr. by William Farrer (Edinburgh: T. & T. Clark, 1850). There is a new translation and edition of this work by John Knox Press.

4. This generally means Hebrew religion in Schleiermacher's use of it. Cf. *On Religion: Speeches to Its Cultured Despisers,* tr. by

John Oman (Harper Torchbook, The Cloister Library; Harper & Row, Publishers, Inc., 1959), pp. 238 ff.

5. Richard R. Niebuhr, *Schleiermacher on Christ and Religion* (Charles Scribner's Sons, 1964), pp. 142–143.

6. *The Meaning and End of Religion*, p. 47.

7. Herrmann, *Gesammelte Aufsätze*, p. 118.

8. *Ibid.*, pp. 95–188.

9. For example, Van A. Harvey, *The Historian and the Believer* (The Macmillan Company, 1966), pp. 128–130.

10. For an account of this consensus religion of America, see Sidney E. Mead, *The Lively Experiment* (Harper & Row, Publishers, Inc., 1963).

CHAPTER SIX

1. A parallel to this argument is found in Mircea Eliade's critique of Hegel in *Cosmos and History: The Myth of the Eternal Return*, tr. by Willard R. Trask (Harper Torchbook, The Cloister Library; Harper & Row, Publishers, Inc., 1959), pp. 147–149.

2. Harvey, *op. cit.*, pp. 54–59.

3. It is pertinent, I think, to notice here a difficulty that arises in dealing with H. Richard Niebuhr's *The Meaning of Revelation* (The Macmillan Company, 1941), and its considerable effect upon the American theological scene. In many ways this book and its close sequel, Harvey, *op. cit.*, have an approach resembling the work of Herrmann. Faith and self-awareness are brought closely together; an openness of spirit in faith is nurtured; and a sensitivity to the tradition that produces faith is recognizable. However, faith is brought into connection with revelation, and the problem of revelation in history is examined from the side of its place in human knowing. This seems to me to introduce the problems for both faith and its expression in historical life entailed in the Johannine provenance.

4. *The Future of Belief: Theism in a World Come of Age* (Herder & Herder, Inc., 1966), pp. 135–151.

5. I would understand this as an extension of the questions raised by Herbert Braun, " The Problem of a New Testament Theology," tr. by Jack Sanders, *Journal for Theology and the Church*, Vol. I, pp. 169–183.